Valuable Driving Tips

A comprehensive Natural Learning Process
Teaching Essentials For Everyday Driving
to improve highway safety.

Vehicle crashes and collisions are caused therefore, they are preventable.

In tribute to our fallen public safety officers, who have lost their life in the line of duty protecting our highway safety!

Visit Valuable Driving Tips @

www.vdt-info.com

Revised Edition © copyright 2011

Understanding the Reality of Driving Through a Natural Learning Process

This Book Covers Highway Safety Rules and some Traffic Laws Which Are Applicable Throughout The United States and Canada.

Illustrated by Ralph Moore

Valuable Driving Tips

Is an Independent Advanced Drivers Instructional Manual, and a Front Runner in Driving Awareness Education for All Drivers Based on Common Sense Driving Rules for Easy Learning. Valuable Driving Tips is a preferred choice to enhance your driving skills and help make our highways safer for all drivers.

For the Beginning Driver...

It's bursting with safe driving knowledge.

For the Experienced Driver...

It's a much needed refresher course.

For the Professional Driver...

It's a wakeup call!

We have included some vital highway statistics to show the need for improving highway safety. Valuable Driving Tips has been reviewed by professional safety officials, transportation authorities, and is recommended for the betterment of public highway safety.

VALUABLE DRIVING TIPS

We believe all qualified drivers are responsible for their own actions while at the wheel of any vehicle traveling our public highways.

VDT may be the first drivers instructional manual to suggest when a person is engaged in a phone conversation either by text or audio while driving, the person to whom the driver is in conversation with should have some responsibility if there is a collision.

No part of this publication may be reproduced, stored in a retrieval system, or transmitted in any form or by any means, electronic, mechanical, photocopying, recording, scanning, or otherwise, except as permitted under Section 107 or 108 of the 1976 United States Copyright Act, without the prior written permission of the Author. Requests to the Author for permission should be addressed to Valuable Driving Tips, P.O. Box 857, Lineville, AL 36266. Or, requests may be made by email at ralphmoore08@gmail.com. You may also visit our web site at WWW.VALUABLEDRIVINGTIPS.COM.

Limit of Liability/Disclaimer of Warranty: **The Valuable Driving Tips book is in no way claiming to have all the answers for safe driving. The contents herein have been compiled from many years of coast to coast driving experiences, observation of general traffic flow, and witness to numerous traffic collisions. We've also included some important information taken from the State of Alabama Department of Highway Safety as well as various data gathered from driving and highway-safety related web sites.**

While the publisher and author have used their best efforts in preparing this book, some of these illustrations may not have not

VALUABLE DRIVING TIPS

been certified or scientifically proven; however, they do represent a reality of everyday driving and common sense safety rules that all drivers will experience. They make no representations or warranties with respect to the accuracy or completeness of the contents of this book and specifically disclaim any implied warranties of merchantability or fitness for a particular purpose. No warranty may be created or extended by sales representatives or written sales materials. The advice and strategies contained herein may not be suitable for your situation. This book, Valuable Driving Tips, is written to provide general educational information about driving and to teach common sense rules and road laws. **It is for a wide audience of drivers and is not intended to provide specific advice to a certain individual driver.** The rules and road laws vary from state to state and can change over time. **You should consult your state-issued Driver's Manual to become familiar with your local laws and highway signage. Neither the publisher nor author shall be liable for any loss, loss of profit, or any other damages, including but not limited to special, incidental, consequential, or other damages**

Some of these illustrations may not be required by law; however, they are common sense and highway safety rules. When put into practice they can help make our highways work more efficiently and be safer for all.

Any time someone drives on the open road, there is a risk involved. There is no way anyone can guarantee highway safety.

VALUABLE DRIVING TIPS

<u>Our illustrations are presented to help make the general danger of driving more recognizable.</u>

FOR YOUR INFORMATION

This book is not the official state driver's manual booklet. However, it does take driving instructions a step beyond the state requirements. It contains common sense rules and actions that can be very helpful in achieving ones goal of becoming a safer, more successful and courteous driver. Whether you will be driving for pleasure or your dream is to become a professional large vehicle operator, this book may have many of the answers necessary to gain that successful position.

Good, responsible driving comes from quality training. One is not born with the proper knowledge of driving. Everyone must have training and general driving instructions in order to become responsible for themselves and others.

ORGAN DONOR ENCOURAGEMENT

Donation of vital organs and tissues can save lives where no other hope is available. Heart, liver, lung and kidney transplants save lives every day. Additionally, bone, skin and cornea transplants often restore sight and save burn victims. Today, through the miracle of transplantation, many people all across the country are living healthy, productive lives. There are thousands more who could be helped if more of us became organ and tissue donors. Organ and tissue donations provide us with a special opportunity to help others. Mark your license and be a donor.

VALUABLE DRIVING TIPS

VALUABLE DRIVING TIPS PERSPECTIVE

Over the past few years, respectful driving has decreased and highway casualties have increased. This is largely attributed to the increase of the use of drugs and alcohol among our young drivers. This fact must change if we are to see our youngsters become successful adults.

We must start by improving our driver education and enforcement of traffic laws. Most important of all, parents must support those laws when their children are caught violating them.

 Young drivers are more likely to have an automobile collision during the first 18 months of their independent driving experience. This is a time when their over-confidence can overpower their ability.

Even in our most advanced efforts to help our young people understand the importance of having a safe and proper driving record, too often they are totally unaware of the serious consequences of creating a bad driving record. A poor record induced with alcohol, drugs, or just plain carelessness could lead to jail time or even a more serious charge.

In later years they may wish to travel abroad, or get that all important job and the bad record you create while in your youth may hinder your ability to achieve any of these goals or opportunities. A bad record created while you think you are having a good time could stay with you your whole lifetime.

A good driving record is just as important as having a good academic record. Here in our Valuable Driving Tips book we hope to create a better understanding of driving among our youth as well as the adults. Improvements in your skills can saves lives.

Our goal is to help make our highways safer for all highway users by bringing a few simple rules and traffic laws to the attention of all drivers, which will help make our roads safer.

RESPECT: THE FIRST STEP IN BECOMING A RESPONSIBLE DRIVER

The first step in learning good driving manners begins with having respect for other drivers who have the same rights to the highways as you do.

We must always have respect for our law enforcement officers whether they are representing city, county, or state agencies.

VALUABLE DRIVING TIPS

These are the men and women who are trained to be on alert for our safety. Without their presence on our highways our lives would be in more danger. Whatever the necessity may be their work never ends. Their lives are on the line for us every working hour. For all they do, I am grateful. I appreciate all their efforts on my behalf and for all other drivers. I know they are doing a very necessary job that I cannot do. **Thank you all for being there!**

"We Remember the Officers"

We remember the officers who changed our lives,
The men and women who protect us day and night,
People who we respect for their dedication to the cause,
For when faced with danger, they never pause.

We remember the officers who always stood true,
Whatever the color of uniform, brown, gray, or blue,
With pride and integrity they say "To serve and protect"
For the giving of their life, we offer our respect.

We remember the officers who we never really knew,
Persons strong enough to answer the challenge are few,
With heavy hearts we mourn the officers in eternal rest,
There's more to these people than the badge on their chest.
- Brad Miller

Thank you Brad Miller for allowing us to use your poem!

VALUABLE DRIVING TIPS

VALUABLE DRIVING TIPS

VALUABLE DRIVING TIPS

**PART SIX---Automobile responsibility & equipment requirements
Pages 86 thru 104**

VALUABLE DRIVING TIPS

Current driving expectations.

PART ONE

THINGS THAT SHOULD NEVER HAPPEN WHILE DRIVING

Some automobile makers suggest that their vehicles are smooth enough to put on your makeup while driving. This is foolish, and you will only see a foolish person attempting this act. Don't risk your safety, and the safety of others, with one-handed driving, and 10% concentration.

TEXTING WHILE DRIVING

With today's technological advancements, there are always new personal electronic devices on the market for listening to music or, communicating with your friends. One of the major causes of teenage deaths is the use of these electronic devices while driving. Are they so important that we are willing to risk our lives, and the lives of others for what we consider convenience? **Your personal electronic devices should not be used while you are driving.**

With all the advanced technology your personal devices have, your online conversations could steal your focus and concentration from your driving responsibility.

 A new study shows a staggering 80% of all car crashes, and 65% of near misses, are caused by distracted drivers more focused on their burgers and phones than the road.

When texting and driving, receiving or sending a text message, you are not looking at the road ahead although you may believe you are being very alert.   In approximately four seconds, driving 55-60

mph, your vehicle can travel 500 feet or more without you realizing it. That's almost like driving blindfolded.

<u>Never</u> use your cell phone or send or receive text messages while driving. These effects can be as tragic as driving under the influence of drugs or alcohol

 In 2009, 5,474 people were killed in the U.S. because of collisions that involved distracted driving. Another 448,000 were injured.

Always have your sunglasses and other driving necessities within comfortable reach. Never attempt to reach for, or search for, these objects while driving. Reaching to retrieve an object may cause you to pull on the steering wheel without realizing you are doing so. Six main reasons for automobile crashes are: speed, alcohol, drugs, distractions, failing to yield, and over active passengers.

While the vehicle is in motion riders must keep head, arms and legs inside the vehicle. Also, don't allow debris to build up in the floor on the driver's side of the vehicle.

NOTE: Current statistics from the AAA Foundation for Traffic Safety: Distracted driving contributes to up to 8,000 crashes every single day – the facts speak for themselves:

- More than one million people have died in car crashes over the past 25 years in the U.S., with 33,788 lives lost in 2010 alone.
- Drivers spend more than half their time behind the wheel engaged in distracted behavior.
- Using a cell phone while driving quadruples your risk of crashing.

- Eating, smoking, adjusting music or rubbernecking while driving can be just as dangerous as texting, emailing or talking on a cell phone.
- Passengers are one of the most frequently reported causes of distraction, with young children being four times more distracting than adults and infants being eight times more distracting.

A majority of drivers – 92% – agree that texting or emailing while driving is unacceptable and 80% support laws against reading, typing or sending text messages or emails while driving, yet a quarter of drivers reported texting or emailing while driving in just recent months. This "do as I say, not as I do" attitude is one of the greatest obstacles preventing us from improving safety on our roads.[i]

LEGAL AGE TO DRIVE

In many states a fifteen year old may qualify to get a driver's learning permit. This achievement will give one the opportunity to drive in traffic and on the open road while under the supervision of a licensed adult.

I would strongly recommend only the beginner driver and the licensed adult supervisor be allowed in the car while in the learning process.

WARNING: In almost every state it is a third-degree felony to use false or fictitious names on any application for a driver's license or identification card; or to knowingly make a false statement, or knowingly conceal a material fact; or otherwise commit a fraud in any such application.

THE DRIVER'S WRITTEN TEST

The written test may be taken in a number of different languages. However, one must be able to read and understand English well enough to obey road signs and general traffic instructions in order to drive safely and defensively on U.S. highways.

THE PRIVILEGE TO OPERATE A VEHICLE

When youngsters get a driver's license at the age of sixteen, or any beginning age, they automatically believe they have achieved an expert status at driving a vehicle. They may spend twelve years going to school to learn enough to graduate, yet they believe they will learn all there is to know about driving an automobile in only a few short days. Studies show it takes 5-10 years, or 50.000 miles of driving to make the average person a responsible driver.

Parents should become more concerned and involved with their inexperienced young drivers. For the most part they are only interested in their youngsters passing the driving test, falsely believing that passing this simple test gives them all the driving knowledge they need. Then they turn them loose to drive by trial and error. Some parents believe if their child has Drivers Education at school he or she is automatically qualified to drive. Not so! Drivers Education only prepares one to learn.

The driver's license only gives one the legal right to learn to drive without the presence of an adult. Teenage death statistics are proof we should become more concerned about our young drivers and their passengers.

Parents will often spend extra money to purchase a higher quality vehicle they believe to be safer in case of a crash, while never considering to provide better driving instruction for the driver. No matter how safe you think the vehicle may be, it may not be safe enough to protect the driver and passengers from driving ignorance.

Many teenage lives can be saved every year by simply limiting how many passengers they are allowed to carry while in their first two years of training. This is a very uncertain time when they are most likely to take unnecessary risks while in the developing stages of their driving skills. Liability in all aspects should be considered.

Many teen drivers think, by taking risks and driving fast, they prove they are a good driver. In fact, they are proving they are not mature enough to drive and are not ready to be allowed to drive unsupervised.

Foolish driving is when you drive in such a way that only proves you are not mature enough to drive in the first place! These drivers are commonly referred to as a "show-off" driver and they are one of the leading causes of automobile collisions.

These are drivers with whom we should refuse to ride with regardless of how good of a friend he or she may be. **You can always be the "smartest" person in the crowd by not allowing your friends to convince you to drive beyond your ability! It's your life so protect it!**

While there are a few exceptions to theses fact, the majority of new drivers place themselves and others at risk every day as they travel and learn.

THE RESPONSIBLE DRIVER

I have had the privilege of seeing a few of today's young people growing up just as I did living in the country on a working farm. These very fortunate youngsters grow up learning to operate farm equipment and drive farm tractors and farm trucks. By the time they reach the legal driving age they are already experienced by several years beyond the average beginner.

These farm-grown kids are almost always respectful drivers, and they usually take care of their "first ride" because it is the one they had to work hard to get. From the beginning, it is just as easy to develop good driving habits as it is to fall into bad ones. Always buckle your seat belt before you start the engine. You should also always check to see that your passengers have buckled up and are secure so as not to interfere with your responsibility of driving.

The person who has slipped under the steering wheel has put him or herself into a responsible position. He or she is responsible for the vehicle and the passengers. Regardless of what activities may be going on inside the vehicle, drivers must never shift their attention from their driving responsibilities to become part of that activity.

Always practice good posture at the steering wheel. This will allow you to be in better control in case of an emergency. You should use both hands on the steering wheel using a firm, but light grip.

Always drive using your right foot only for acceleration and braking. Your left foot should stay on the floor while you are driving or coming to a stop. Use the left foot for the clutch if you are driving a manual transmission. **Never use your left foot for breaking or acceleration.**

The driver must always be focused on the road ahead. He must watch his speed as well as the speed of all other vehicles close to him. The driver must always watch out for other drivers who may not be as alert as they should be. Often times when meeting another vehicle, you may notice it may drift to the center line or gets too close to the right shoulder of the road.

These situations often happens when the driver is preoccupied with cell phones, food, cigarettes, maps, or involved in conversation within the vehicle. It only takes a second for your vehicle to wonder out of control. Passengers should never involve the driver in heated conversation while the vehicle is in motion. **Distractions remain one of the greatest causes of automobile crashes.**

A SAFE DRIVER IS MATURE ALERT AND IN CONTROL

Many factors, including those already mentioned, play a deadly role in highway casualties. One should not drive when mad or upset. Too often one will use the vehicle to express their anger. Your temperament can also affect your driving ability.

We live in a "quick" driving society. We start off quickly, stop quickly, and get upset when all other drivers don't do the same. Get in touch with reality; slow down, relax, and share the road.

If you become sleepy or tired while driving, you should find a safe place to stop and get refreshed before continuing your journey. If you continue to drive trying to fight sleep, it is very easy to become hypnotized by the road sounds and seeing the dotted highway lines slip past your vehicle. One can become dazed, and actually be dreaming, and be convinced that it is ok to take a quick nap even though they may be driving 60 miles per hour. Many lives have been lost because of this action. .

Rest is the only cure for fatigue. Just paying attention and staying alert can prevent many crashes. Keeping the vehicle cooler may also help prevent drowsiness.

THE UNCONCERNED DRIVER

One of the things I have noticed in observing some young drivers is that it seems as if they think they are the only ones on the road. They are fixed in their position at the wheel almost as if they are frozen with their hands at the 10 and 2 position and their eyes focused directly ahead. They will travel through an intersection with almost no thought of any other vehicle being there. Their speed is usually much greater than it should be for the road conditions and their level of experience. If the traffic light changes to red, they hit the brakes suddenly throwing the nose of the vehicle toward the ground. When the light turns green they accelerate just as rapidly as they came to a stop. This is neither a normal nor safe way to drive. We should approach every intersection with caution as though someone may run the stop light or stop sign. **Use peripheral vision and stay alert.**

As a beginning driver, you should train yourself to stay alert. Your eyes should always be scanning the intersection as well as the oncoming traffic approaching from either side of your right of way. Always expect that unconcerned driver to run the light or the stop sign. **Just because you may have the right of way does not always mean the other driver will know, or respect, that fact.**

When you are at a signal light-controlled intersection, and you are waiting for the light to turn green, you should always look both ways before you begin to move forward. Moving ahead too quickly could result in a collision with that impatient driver who fails to respect the yellow light. You should always stay alert at these intersections. Use common sense before over accelerating.

Try to avoid window shopping while you are stopped. This will prevent the driver behind you from calling your attention to the green light. Patience saves time and lives. **Nearly fifty percent of all automobile crashes are caused by someone running a stop sign or traffic light, or failing to yield the right of way.** We must realize that no time is gained by rushing to beat the changing traffic light.

From a normal starting point, it is not necessary to over accelerate when starting. Over acceleration can cause unnecessary wear on your engine, transmission, and tires as well as decrease your fuel economy.

DISRESPECTFUL DRIVERS

A common scene of driver disrespect is a vehicle, large or small, trapped in the left lane of the highway traffic with the right turn signal blinking, indicating the need to move into the right lane. Rapidly passing vehicles are disregarding the signaling vehicle and forcefully passing without giving thought, or concern, for the trapped motorist. **An astonishing 80% of four-wheel vehicle drivers are guilty of this act.** Why are we in such a disrespectful hurry?

DO WE REWARD OUR TEENAGERS FOR RECKLESS DRIVING

How many times have we known of a teenager who has wrecked or totaled their vehicle because of foolish and reckless driving? Many times the victims of the automobile crash are in the hospital with life threatening conditions. However, the problem lies within the fact that even though the teenager wrecks their vehicle and puts themselves or others in the hospital, as soon as they recover, they will be given another vehicle. Sometimes it will even be newer than the one they have wrecked! To me, this looks like a reward for reckless driving. In many cases parents take the bicycle away much too soon.

From the onset of their driving experiences, we need to teach our young drivers the dangers of driving instead of the pleasures. The true comfort and pleasure of driving can only come when we clearly understand the dangers.

Too many drivers think nothing of driving. It is just something most teens think they are entitled to when they reach the driving age. They seem to believe driving just comes naturally and no problems will arise.

Sometime, when you are out and about, take notice of how many vehicles you see that have come in contact with another vehicle or other objects. Peep over the fence of a local junkyard and this will give you an idea of how many drivers think there is "nothing to it." There are nearly as many wrecked cars in the junk yard as there are cars for sale on car lots.

What the teens and many of their parents don't take seriously is they are about to be in control of a 3,000 to 4,000 pound deadly weapon. A teen cannot use a gun to go hunting without passing a Hunter's Safety course, but they are allowed to take a 2-ton, high-speed vehicle on the road by merely demonstrating only the most basic maneuvers at low speed! In most cases more time is spent teaching one to ride a bicycle than is spent teaching one to drive a vehicle.

We lock up our gun cabinets and place the key in a secure place, Then, we hand over the car keys to an inexperienced, and sometimes, thoughtless young driver.

Many times parents are so excited about getting the first ride for their children they often forget they are still just kids.

We often hear our leaders speak of gun control, yet automobile drivers kill more people than guns. Who among our leaders is saying anything about improving our driving skills? We have come to accept highway casualties as a natural cause of death when, in fact, they are preventable.

FACTS ABOUT DRINKING, DRIVING AND DRUGS

Here is a staggering fact: the leading causes of teenage deaths are automobile collisions. It has been well documented that automobile crashes are responsible for approx. 40,000 fatalities every year in the United States! Many of these victims are inexperienced and irresponsible teenage drivers.

NOTE: Every day, APPROXIMATELY 40 young driver's ages 16-19, are killed in crashes and another 745 are injured!

- About 25% of crashes killing young drivers involve alcohol.

- 39% of young male drivers and 26% of young female drivers were speeding at the time of their fatal crash.

- Although young drivers only represent 6% of all licensed drivers, they are the drivers in 16% of all traffic crashes.[ii]

FATAL TEEN CRASH STATISTICS

Motor vehicle crashes are the leading cause of death for U.S. teens, accounting for more than one in three deaths in this age group. Among teen drivers, those at especially high risk of crashing are:

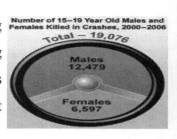

Number of 15–19 Year Old Males and Females Killed in Crashes, 2000–2006
Total – 19,076
Males 12,479
Females 6,597

Males: From 2000 to 2006, the number of male drivers and passengers ages 15 to 19 who were killed in crashes was higher

(12,479) than the number of female drivers and passengers who were killed (6,579).[iii]

Teens driving with teen passengers: Driving with teen passengers increases the crash risk of unsupervised teen drivers. This risk increases with the number of teen passengers.

Driving at night statistics show the crash risks for teen driving at night is nearly twice as high as the crash risks during the day.

Newly licensed teens: Crash risk is highest during the first year that teens are eligible to drive.

Drugs, alcohol and speed are the leading causes of automobile collisions.

High speed, following too closely, and driver inexperience are some of the reasons for highway collisions. However, the most devastating cause of automobile crashes is the detrimental impact of alcohol and drugs. **Young people who drink and drive may be particularly at risk for being involved in a motor vehicle collision because they have less experience with driving and are more likely to engage in risk-taking behavior.**

DRIVING GAMES & ENTERTAINING PASSENGERS

An automobile can be a lot of fun yet, for any beginning driver, it can also be very dangerous. We must always be concerned when there is an inexperienced or careless driver at the wheel. Too often, young or inexperienced drivers think they are in full control of their speeding vehicle when, in fact, high speed can steal their ability to control the vehicle without them realizing the dangerous situation until it is too late.

While the vehicle is in motion, passengers should never tease the driver by pulling on the steering wheel, the switch keys, gear selector or emergency brakes. This foolish action can lead to serious consequences.

Almost every young driver has found a dip in the road or a quick drop on a hill, which they call a "Thrill Hill." They **_all_** want to take their friends for a ride on this special spot. These kinds of conditions, coupled with too much speed, can result in losing control of the vehicle and causing much damage and most likely causing injury to themselves as well.

VALUABLE DRIVING TIPS

When high speed and reckless driving becomes your entertainment you are already in trouble. It is very easy to understand the thrill of power at your command, and it is easy to get excited when that powerful engine responds to your foot pressing the accelerator. However, we must always respect that power and use it only when needed in order to get out of a dangerous situation.

Those who enjoy the fast ride should be wary of the overall weight of their speeding vehicle. **Even with the aerodynamic design, at the speed of 80-100 M.P.H., your vehicle could become light enough on the ground to be lifted by one man.** At this high rate of speed, any simple road hazard could cause your vehicle to become uncontrollably airborne. **The greater your speed becomes, the lighter your automobile becomes; therefore, your ability to stay in full control is drastically reduced.** "Think" before you become a victim of your own foolish driving games.

Always remember, passengers are no safer than the driving ability and driving experience of the driver.

Drag racing, for example, should be done only on designated drag strips. **Unauthorized drag racing is very dangerous and unlawful. It should never be done on any public street or highway.** These games could result in the loss of life or permanent bodily injuries. To challenge a friend with the strength of an automobile is very foolish. Sometimes a word from a true friend can prevent these actions.

A public highway is no place to play. If you must prove how well you can drive by driving fast or reckless, perhaps you are too immature to drive at all. Any driver can drive fast, but it is always more impressive to drive with control and awareness.

Most young people, and some who are not so young, will tell you they love to drive fast; however, we must remember, most of the single vehicle collisions happen because of high speed. The faster you drive, the less thinking time you have in case of an emergency.

These driving games can cause you to swerve onto the shoulder of the road or drift across the center line of a highway, your actions could become reactions, which often results in the loss of control of your vehicle. 'The momentum' caused by the speed of your vehicle can overpower your ability to control it in an emergency situation.

Driving is not like the famous burger place, you can't always have it your way. You must blend with traffic and comply with traffic laws.

 Most drivers are convinced they are perfect drivers because they taught themselves. For the most part this is why, in America today; automobile collisions are a

leading cause of death. Earn the respect of your peers and
others by driving responsibly.

FAMILY FUN CAN RESULT IN TRAGEDY

Family vacations are great! However, too many times they end in
tragedy. Sometimes, even the best we can do is not enough.
Before you know it, someone has made a mistake and caused an
automobile collision. Unfortunately, Alabama is one of the top
states in terms of highway casualties. Many times as I travel on

old US 431 in Southeast Alabama, I am reminded of the highway danger by the many white crosses along a short stretch of that highway. Although I did not know any of these victims personally, I can imagine many of them were young people on their way to the beach or on their way home. Perhaps they were excited about their trip and the automobile was filled with laughter as they rounded curve after curve. Maybe their speed began to build with the anticipation of getting to their desired location as quickly as possible. We must always remember there will be time to play after we have arrived at our destination.

HIGHWAY DEATHS ARE PREVENTABLE

Every 15 minutes, someone in the United States learns that a loved one has been injured or has died in an automobile crash. Every day, 119 people die on American roads and highways. That's more than 40,000 every year! **We must stop accepting highway causalities as a natural cause of death. Highway deaths are preventable. Drive Responsibly!**

If one teenager leaves home for a time of fun with friends and never returns, that is an "unforgettable tragedy!"

Every year, more than 13,000 teenagers leave home under the same pretense, never to return. That is an "unacceptable tragedy!"

PART TWO

STATE REQUIREMENTS

In order to drive an automobile legally on US highways, the following equipment must be in proper working order: lights, windshield wipers, horn, brakes, exhaust system, rearview mirror, tag light, and tires.

LIABILITY INSURANCE LAW

Most states have a mandatory liability insurance law. Proof of all automobile insurance must be carried in the vehicle at all times.

Basic auto liability insurance policies consist of two types of benefits or coverage including coverage for bodily injury and property damage. Bodily injury liability provides protection from various claims and court cases that are filed against insured persons in case the insured person is the cause of injury or death of another person. This type of coverage pays costs for the affected person or their relatives for the pain, suffering, and other hardships, and also for economic damages.

RESPECTING AND OBEYING ROAD SIGNS

Regulatory	Information	Warning
Warning	Warning	Information
Warning	Regulatory	Warning
Warning	Regulatory	Regulatory

Driving is a very serious responsibility and should always be respected as such. As you learn to drive, you should also learn to observe all road signs. When you are studying for your written exam you will read about these signs and see diagrams of them in your driver's manual. Now that you are driving, these signs become a reality and must be respected as such. Learn the shape and color of the most common road signs.

There are three types of traffic signs. They are as follows: warning, regulatory, and information.

"Stop" A stop sign means just that—"STOP." **You should come to a complete stop and look both ways to be sure the right of way is clear before proceeding into the roadway.**

"Yield" means, for safety, slow down to 10-15 miles per hour and be prepared to stop so you can yield the right of way to any pedestrian or oncoming vehicles before entering the normal flow of traffic. **The yield sign is not a green light. You must stop if there is any other vehicle within or approaching the intersection or highway you are merging into. The approaching vehicle has the right of way.** That yield sign also pertains to a pedestrian in a crosswalk. This is a warning sign.

"Wrong Way" means you are going in the wrong direction. When you are entering a highway and you see this sign, you should stop immediately, turn around and get out of this dangerous situation.

"Do Not Enter" signs serve the same purpose. You are about to be traveling in the wrong direction.

"No Parking" signs are posted to secure an area. Sometimes it may be a yellow, red or blue curb. It may indicate "Reserved for the Handicapped," or "Emergency Vehicles Only." Just as a stop signs mean "Stop", a no parking signs means "No Parking".

Now that you are driving, you are in the position to see, obey, and learn firsthand the importance of these signs. **There is a reason these signs are placed out there on the highways. These signs make unfamiliar places easier to travel through and are there for your safety.** Sure, there may be places where these signs may read "Curvy Road Ahead", "35 M.P.H.", and you may be able to take these curves at 50 M.P.H. However, this is never a wise choice to make. You should never challenge these conditions! One can never correctly estimate what is just around the curve or just over the next hill or about the condition of the road ahead.

SPEED LIMITS

Speed causes many crashes. More drivers are convicted of speeding than any other offense. To avoid being fined or involved in a crash, obey the speed limits. Speed is very detrimental in a collision. If you double the speed of a car, you increase its force of impact four times. If you triple the speed, the impact is nine times as great.

 Speed limit signs _are not_ posted to tell you how fast you must drive: they are there to tell you the maximum speed you are allowed to drive without violating the speed law. To exceed the speed limit is to neglect safety.

70 does not always mean 70. Remember that speed limits show the fastest speed you may drive under good conditions. You are responsible for adjusting your driving speed to the road conditions. For example, if the weather is bad or there is a lot of traffic, you must drive more slowly than the posted speed. The slower speed is the one that allows you to have better control of your vehicle and avoid collisions with other vehicles.

One of the most disrespected mandatory sign on the road is one that reads "Speed Zone Ahead". Speed limit signs are posted at the beginning of a speed zone and drivers must be driving at that speed starting at the location of the posted sign and continuing until there is a posted speed limit change. This sign "Speed Zone Ahead" means, when you see it, take your foot off the accelerator and allow your vehicle to slow down on its own. By the time you reach the posted speed zone you will most likely be traveling the correct speed without applying your brakes.

Speed limits may vary from state to state. The most commonly posted speeds are 30 M.P.H. in an urban district, 35 M.P.H. on unpaved roads, and 40 M.P.H. **on county paved roads. If the speed limit is not posted on a county paved road you should assume that it is 40 M.P.H.**

On state highways, it is usually 55 M.P.H. unless it is interstate or highways with 4 lanes. On interstate highways the speed limit is 70 M.P.H. unless otherwise posted.

LEFT-LANERS

Another form of disrespect is abusing the left-most lane. This is not only unsafe but is also very disrespectful to drivers who are traveling at a higher rate of speed than you.

Many people think multi-lane roads are made so that two or three cars can drive side-by-side at the same speed. That's NOT what they are designed to do. They are designed to

handle a higher flow of traffic and to keep the traffic moving as efficiently as possible.

Two cars driving side-by-side at the same speed is great if you're leading a parade; not so when you are traveling on a multi-lane highway!

Many states have a road law and even road signs that say "SLOWER TRAFFIC KEEP RIGHT" and/or "KEEP RIGHT EXCEPT TO PASS". Think of this as one of the Golden Rules of highway driving!

If you are in the left lane and another driver is approaching from behind at a higher rate of speed, look to see if it is safe to change lanes. Then, you should signal and move to the right lane; or, if you and the car traveling beside you are staying side-by-side, the car in the left lane should speed up or slow down and get behind, or in front of the car to the right. It makes a highway work much more efficiently!

Don't be a disrespectful Left-Laner!

MOVE OVER LAW

An expanded "Move-over America" law provides an added measure of safety for emergency responders stopped or parked roadside with emergency signals activated.

The newly enhanced law adds wreckers to emergency response vehicles for which motorists must move over one lane. When moving over is unsafe or not possible, such as on two-lane roadways, motorists must slow down to 20 mph below the posted speed limit. A six-month warning and educational period for the new law began Aug. 1, 2007. Once the warning period concluded, citations for violation of the "move-over" law will carry a fine of up to $25 for first offense and increasing fines for second and subsequent offenses.

 When we see flashing lights on the roadway up ahead, we should approach with caution. When possible, move over to the next lane.

For safety reasons, any time a vehicle is parked alongside the highway, you should approach with caution and move over if possible.

RESPECTING EMERGENCY VEHICLES

One of the largest issues in traffic is the lack of understanding of what the flashing red lights and/or the sound of a siren means. We have all been taught to "Stop for the emergency vehicle" and that fact will not change. However, *"**where** do we stop"* is the question!

When we hear or see an emergency vehicle approaching, we should start looking for a way to help clear the right of way. Most of the time just pulling over and stopping is the right thing to do.

The sound of a siren or the sight of flashing red or blue lights causes some people to panic. They will come to a complete stop in the middle of traffic as though they have no idea what to do. Almost every emergency vehicle operator will tell you he or she sees this confusion every day.

Yield to the lane adjacent to the emergency vehicle and stop. The sound of the siren and the sight of flashing red lights mean that you should do your part to clear the right of way, even if it means turning off your direct route to get your vehicle out of the path of the emergency vehicle.

Along the same lines, blue lights are usually seen on law enforcement vehicles. These blue lights must be respected as well. If you are caught breaking any traffic laws, when you see these lights behind you, you are already caught. Your tag number, as well as the make and model of your vehicle, has been recorded by the officer's dashboard camera and/or reported by radio. For anyone to try to escape at this point would be foolish.

A foolish action would only make your situation much worse. At the same time, you would be placing yourself and others in extreme danger.

PART THREE
RUBBERNECKING

Rubbernecking describes the act of gawking at something of interest. It is often used to refer to drivers trying to view the carnage resulting from a traffic collision. The term refers to the craning of a person's neck in order to get a better view. Rubbernecking has also been described as a human trait that is associated with morbid **curiosity**.

Never slow down on a busy highway just to get a closer look at the emergency situation. This is very dangerous because of the fact that until the scene of a car crash is cleared away a dangerous phenomenon known as "rubbernecking" often occurs.

Rubbernecking too often occurs on a divided highway when the emergency is in the opposite direction lanes of traffic. **We should keep moving at a normal pace when the emergency situation or traffic condition has nothing to do with our direction of traffic.** Passing motorists slow down considerably to observe the after math of a collision, or curious bystanders form a crowd around the site. Rubbernecking can be a very dangerous practice, especially for those who must negotiate both the original crash scene, and the traffic congestion created by curious gawkers.

Emergency officials at crash scenes often try to discourage rubbernecking by forcefully directing drivers to keep moving. Always keep moving with the flow of traffic. This action could avoid an additional collision at the same site.

ROAD RAGED DRIVERS

THIS IS MY LANE STAY OUT OF IT

Who are they and why do they become so impatient when someone doesn't drive to suit them? They will usually sound their horns to let you know their whereabouts. Then, when they have your attention they will point to the sky with an upraised middle finger. This signal means, **"I am an aggressive driving idiot so get out of my lane."**

When one of these people has exposed themself to you, you should give a driving signal, not reciprocate the signal given you, and attempt to move to the next lane allowing them space. **These people are called "Road Raged Drivers".**

'Road rage' **is aggressive or angry behavior by a driver of an automobile or other motor vehicles.** Such behavior might include rude gestures, verbal insults, deliberately driving in an unsafe or threatening manner, or making threats. Road rage can lead to altercations, assaults, and collisions which result in injuries and even death. It can be thought of as an extreme case of <u>aggressive driving</u>. The term originated in the United States during the 1980s, specifically from Newscasters at KTLA a local television station in Los Angeles, California. The term originated in 1987-1988, where a rash of freeway shootings occurred on the 405, 110 and 10

freeways in Los Angeles. These shooting sprees even spawned a response from the AAA Motor Club to its members on how to respond to drivers with road rage or aggressive maneuvers and gestures. **Always remember: Never engage these drivers in confrontation. Their brain does not appear to work in a normal capacity.** They must be unhappy in some way and they take their problems out on innocent people who have the audacity to be in their vicinity. Therefore, allow them space to move on while you enjoy your driving. That's how I see it

THE EXPRESSWAY IS NO PLACE TO LEARN TO DRIVE

The freeway is a different world when it comes to driving. There are multiple lanes of traffic, more signage, minimum speed limits, and things happening on all four sides of your vehicle. This is NO place for beginners! Only the experienced driver should venture here.

After one has had enough driving experience to feel comfortable driving on 2-lane and 4-lane rural or small-city roads and is able to maintain a safe steady speed, it is all right to try your hand at driving in the normal flow of expressway traffic. When entering this highway system, you should be prepared to drive at a normal speed to blend with the flow of traffic.

As you enter the express highway system, typically within the first mile, you will find necessary information signs posted that will tell you what interstate highway you have just entered, the direction you are traveling and the posted speed limit.

This signage prevents one from driving many miles in the wrong direction. Observe and obey all posted roads signs.

THE EXPRESSWAY IS A FORCED DRIVING ZONE

For your travel information: The United States Interstate Highway System has a minimum speed limit. The minimum speed is usually forty (40) miles per hour. However, if you are unable to drive at least fifty-five miles per hour in the right lane, you should find an alternate route for safety reasons. **You are never in a safe position when everyone is passing you, whether it is on a four-lane or a two-lane highway.**

Find the lane of traffic which best suits your desired speed. Stay in your lane unless it becomes necessary for you to change lanes. Lane hopping is dangerous. **Never change more than one lane at a time.** When changing lanes on any highway, be sure the desired lane is clear before moving into the next lane. **You should use the doorstep method when changing more than one lane.** Use your signal, be sure your next lane is clear, and then move to the next lane when it has become clear and safe for you to do so.

Whether you are entering the expressway, exiting, or just finding a more suitable speed lane to travel in, a sudden dash across lanes is extremely dangerous and unlawful.

When there are two or more vehicles traveling together, these vehicles should not travel closer than 300 feet. Trying to stay too close together could create a traffic hazard causing everyone to be in danger. This common-sense rule applies to both interstate travel and two-lane highways.

Except in extreme emergencies you should never park on the shoulder of the expressway. If stopping should become necessary pull as far off on the shoulder of the highway as possible. You should always try to avoid stopping alongside a guard rail because it could limit you access to your vehicle, and it could prevent you from opening your passenger door. Be sure to turn on the four-way emergency flashers. This is especially important at night.

You should not trust the taillights to give warning. Many drivers have crashed into the rear of a parked vehicle because they thought it was moving normally. When returning to the flow of traffic, try to build up enough speed so that you are moving into the flow as smoothly as possible.

 If your vehicle has become disabled, make every effort to move the vehicle from the traffic flow lane. If moving the vehicle is not possible, use lighting devices and or flairs to warn other motorist of the existing danger.

THE RAMP

A highway ramp (as in exit ramp and entrance ramp) or *slip road* is a short section of road which allows vehicles to enter or exit a freeway (motorway).

A directional ramp always tends toward the desired direction of travel. This means that a ramp that makes a left turn exits from the left side of the roadway (a left exit). Left directional ramps are relatively uncommon as the left lane is usually reserved for high-speed through traffic. Ramps for a right turn are almost always right directional ramps. Where traffic drives on the left, these cases are reversed.

A non-directional ramp goes in a direction opposite to the desired direction of travel. Many loop ramps (as in a cloverleaf) are non-directional.

A semi-directional ramp exits a road in a direction opposite from the desired direction of travel, but then turns toward the desired direction of travel. Many flyover ramps (as in a stack) are semi-directional.

The entrance ramp is designed to give you the opportunity to build speed as you travel down the ramp. By looking ahead and over your left shoulder you will be able to find your gap in the flow of traffic. Most motorists on the expressway will move over to the next lane to allow the merging traffic to blend in with the normal flow. However, we must always watch out for the unconcerned driver.

As you travel down the ramp toward the traffic flow lanes, you should have your turn signal on to indicate your approach to the traffic. Leave your signal on until you have entered the traffic flow lane.

 ALWAYS REMEMBER: Giving a signal does not give you the right of way. It only indicates your intent. Drive down the ramp with caution and look for a space to blend in with the flow of traffic.

Never stop at the end of the ramp just to wait for a chance to pull into the traffic flow. This action would be almost as critical and dangerous as stopping in the flow of traffic. **However, there may be conditions whereby stopping at the end of the ramp may be**

necessary. **Some of these conditions can be bumper-to-bumper rush-hour traffic, or emergency situation.**

In some inner-city areas with limited ramp space; as you enter the entrance ramp you may notice a white line all the way across the roadway with a stop sign on each side of the road accompanied by another sign which may be black and white that reads: **"WAIT AT WHITE LINE UNTIL THE VEHICLE IN FRONT OF YOU HAS LEFT THE RAMP".**

In some areas a stop-and-go light has been placed here because of too much neglect of the stop and go sign. Overly anxious and impatient drivers have caused numerous rear end collisions on these ramps. Looking ahead and paying attention will avoid many automobile collisions.

Give a break take a break. This is an act of common courtesy in heavy traffic or emergency situations. By showing this courtesy it will allow traffic to move more smoothly and return to a normal flow.

In some areas, these signs bare diagrams to help make your exit simpler. With all this visible information, about 10% of all motorists making these exits change their mind in the last three seconds of the exit. They will dash across lanes in the path of other motorists placing themselves and others in a life threatening position. This lane violation is a serious problem, and it is also unlawful.

 If you find yourself in the wrong exit lane, just follow it through until you can find another exit; then come back to your desired exit.

Never dash across lanes to correct your own mistake. There could be a vehicle in your blind spot which could cause a disaster. Staying alert and paying attention can avoid these dangerous conditions.

Interstate highways are marked clearly from one to five miles in advance of these interchanges.

When you are approaching an interchange, you will find signs which may be placed directly overhead. These signs will help you know which lane you should be in so that you can remain on the highway you are on, or so you can exit onto another highway.

EXIT THE EXPRESSWAY USING CAUTION

Your exit should be a smooth exit with speed great enough so as not to cause other motorists to slow down because of your actions. Be prepared to stop at the end of the exit ramp if necessary.

Some exits may merge into another street or highway. Some may call for a yield, or a common stop sign. Always bring your speed down in order to comply with either of these conditions.

Some exits have a designated deceleration lane as indicated in the following diagram. Some exits go directly off from the traffic lane. If you do not have a deceleration lane, as you reduce your speed, make sure the traffic behind you has recognized your signal and has responded by slowing down or changing lanes. Always slow down to the posted speed of the exit. Interstate highway exits are marked clearly from one to five miles in advance of these interchanges. Always pay attention to the direction you wish to travel. Stay alert, and stay alive.

Valuable Driving Tips--Drive Safe

Know your lane position

 The best highway safety insurance you can have is the space you keep between you and the vehicle in front of you.

FOLLOWING TOO CLOSE

Every day as we travel the streets and highways we see vehicles following too closely to the vehicle in front of them. These are not all teenagers I am speaking about! Some are older, and more experienced drivers who should know better.

 If you can read the tag number on the vehicle in front of you driving at fifty miles per hour — you are too close! Following too closely is a collision waiting to happen!

When you are too close to the vehicle in front of you there is no way for you to drive safely. **At this point it is difficult to see the road ahead and you must rely on the person in the vehicle ahead of you to do your driving for you.** There could be an object in the road ahead that only the person in front of you can see. This thought should cause anyone to back off and not follow too close.

How many times have you heard someone say—"Just let them run into me from the rear, and it will be their fault!" Don't be misled: this is not always true! **If you create the condition by blocking or hindering the flow of traffic, you can be charged with causing a crash.**

Here is a practical way to judge how close you are stopping to the vehicle in front of you. When you are in heavy traffic, stop and go, or stopped for a traffic light, you should keep enough distance between your vehicle and the vehicle in front of you, whereby, you can clearly see both of their back tires with approximately 3 to 4 feet clearance. This gives you enough room so that, for example, if someone coming up behind you can't stop in time, you could get out of that bad situation and not become part of a multi-car pileup!

When following too closely to the vehicle in front of you, you may have the tendency to do as they do such as over correcting or darting off the roadway.

PART FOUR
SPEED VERSES STOPPING DISTANCE

This driver's manual gives an example of how to judge your safe following distance. **Stopping distances will vary depending on many factors, a few of which are the weight of the vehicle, the road and weather conditions, the type and condition of your tires, etc.** If you are preoccupied in a phone conversation or involved in any distraction within the vehicle, you're thinking and reaction time may not be very quick.

Think about this: You can roughly estimate your speed in feet-per-second by using the following formula:

1 mph = 1.4667 feet per second or roughly 1.5 fps

In other words, if you take the number of miles-per-hour and add that to one-half of that same number, you get approximately the number of feet your vehicle will travel in one second.

30 mph + 15 mph (1/2 of 30) = 45 feet per second

At 60 mph we do the same thing. If we take 60, plus half of 60, which is 30, added together means that at 60 M.P.H. we will travel 90 feet in one second. This helps you realize the relationship of speed, time, and distance. It helps you understand why so many people end up in pile-ups.

With the speed of 30 M.P.H., you will have traveled 66 feet before you perceive that you need to stop and your brain reacts and tell your foot to get on the brake pedal and begin to stop. Once your brain and eyes get the message to your foot and your foot stops the wheels you will have traveled another 42.9 feet. This is a total of 108.9 feet before coming to a full stop.

When traveling 35 M.P.H, the perception and reaction distance would be 77 feet, the braking distance of 58.3 feet. The total stopping distance would be 135.3 feet.

When traveling 45 M.P.H. your perception and reaction distance would be 99 feet and the braking distance would be 96.4 feet with a total stopping distance of 195.4 feet.

Traveling 55 M.P.H. your perception and reaction distance would be 121 feet. You would travel another 144 feet before coming to a stop. The total distance traveled will be 265 feet. When we drive too close to the vehicle in front of us, we should think about the response time it would take for us to stop in case of an emergency. The old theory of adding one car link of 20ft for each ten miles per hr. you travel has not been used for many years. This theory was replaced by the two second rule. However, the old theory may still be very effective because the thought of adding 20ft for each ten miles per hour you're traveling created an image in one's mind that caused them to back off and not ride someone's bumper. **Rear end collisions out number all crashes!**

The chart on the next page is to remind drivers of the reaction time and the danger of driving too close to the vehicle in front of you. **The stopping distance from eye to brain, to foot, to wheel, to road is as follows:**

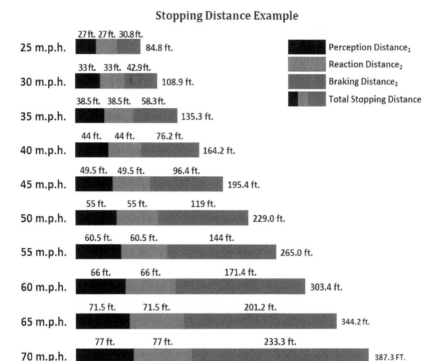

Stopping Distance Example

1. Perception Distance is based on the amount of time it takes for you to perceive there is a reason to stop.
2. Reaction Distance is based on the amount of time it takes for your brain to get your foot on the brake and begin stopping.
3. Braking Distance is the the distance it takes to get your car stopped after the brakes are applied.
Perception Distance and Reaction Distance are based on 0.75 seconds for each.

Here you may notice more than one theory of stopping distances. This is not to contradict or disclaim anyone such theory. Stopping distances will vary depending on many factors. Our goal is to present different angles in hope that at least one of them will be practiced to avoid collisions.

THE TWO SECOND RULE

The following chart illustrates why the two-second rule is more readily adaptable for today's drivers and allows for a safer following distance

CAR SPEED	FEET CAR WILL TRAVEL IN 1 SECOND	AT 1 CAR LENGTH FOR EACH 10 MPH YOU WILL BE: (Bases on a 20 ft. vehicle)	USING THE 2 SECOND RULE YOU WILL BE:
30 mph = 40 mph = 50 mph =	44.4 58.6 73.3	60 ft. back 80 ft. back 100 ft. back	88.8 ft. back 117.2 ft. back 146.6 ft. back

You may have even seen a chart similar to the one above. Perhaps in your state issued driver's manual it describes how the distance between you and the vehicle in front of you may be measured by counting the seconds as you pass a fixed object. **For example: Fix your eyes on an object ahead of the vehicle in front of you. When the vehicle in front of you passes the object, start**

counting. Now, count the seconds until you pass the same object.

You may count the two seconds by saying, "Mississippi 1, Mississippi 2." This phrase makes the two second count.

To me, the visible theory is more effective. One should learn to judge distance at sight. If it is difficult for you to estimate distances, you may practice by thinking about the size of your house or the length of your drive way. You may look at your class room and try to estimate its length and width. How long is the hallway of your school? The football field is always a very good way to help you realize distances. The field is typically 300 feet long; the 50 yard line is half way across the field, which makes 150 feet. A highway exit sign is also a good way to learn how to judge distances. When you are coming to an exit, you may see the exit sign that reads, "Exit one mile" or ¾ miles or ½ mile. These signs help you to be prepared to make your exit. These signs will also help you to learn to judge distance "at a glance." Everyone who drives needs to learn to estimate feet at a glance. It is important for your safety.

COLLISION INVOLVEMENT RULES

If you are involved in an automobile collision, you should stop at once and aid any injured persons. A police report is required for all collisions with 250.00 dollars of damage or any injury. Call for medical assistance if injuries are serious. You should avoid moving any injured victim unless it is necessary to move them to safety from fire, rising water, or any other immediate danger.

You should show your license to the other driver involved in the crash. Giving your name, address, and showing your registration and insurance coverage is your responsibility. Use whatever means available to warn the other traffic of the highway danger. Never leave the scene of an automobile collision until all parties are satisfied with the information exchanged. If you should hit a vacant parked car you should leave your information where the vehicle owner can locate it.

NATIONAL CAR COLLISION STATISTICS

There are more than six million <u>car crashes</u> each year in the United States. A person dies in a car crash every 12 minutes and each year car crashes kill 40,000 people. The leading cause of death for individuals between two and thirty-four years old is motor vehicle crashes.

Someone is injured by a car crash every 14 seconds and about two million of the people injured in car collision each year suffer **permanent injuries.**

Over 25% of all drivers were involved in an automobile crash in a five-year period.

Excessive speed is the second most common cause of deadly automobile crashes, which accounts for about 30% of fatalities.

Car crashes cost each American more than $1,000 a year; $164.2 billion is the total cost each year across the United States. [iv]

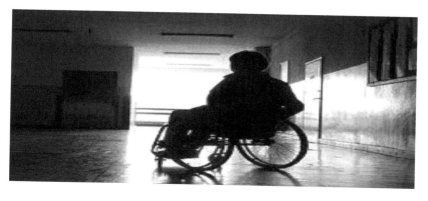

This could be the result of a very unsafe and unlawful act often seen on county, state, and U.S. highways. A driver will pull across the center line to the left side of the road to retrieve their mail from the mailbox. Many times the approaching driver is startled at this unexpected sight and caught completely off guard by a vehicle facing them and taking up part of their travel lane. With this condition thinking time is limited. Many collisions have happened as a result of this lazy and thoughtless act. Park in your driveway and walk a few feet and stay safe.

PART FIVE

ROAD CONDITIONS

As you travel on the secondary roads, you may notice they are not built as smoothly as the interstate highway system. You may also notice dips in the road or uneven pavement. When you are driving the posted speed limit these imperfections in the road come alive and can be felt in your steering wheel. When you exceed the safe speed limit these conditions may become less noticeable. However, they do still exist.

The faster the speed becomes the less road conditions are noticed; but the more dangerous your driving will become. Many times a young or inexperienced driver can lose control of the vehicle instantly in these conditions even though they do not realize they are in any danger.

Unfortunately, too many times this type of thing can happen when there are two or more young people in the same vehicle and less attention is paid to the condition of the road or highway.

WET HIGHWAYS ARE SLIPPERY

Wet highways are more slippery than most drivers realize. As thousands of vehicles travel the roadways, they drip oil and other fluids. When these fluids become mixed with rain, they create an oily and very slick surface on the road.

When traveling down the highway after or during a rain storm we have all seen some vehicle off the road, in a ditch, or in the center median. Sometimes this is caused by those who are overly confident in their driving abilities and fail to respect the road or weather conditions. These scenes are proof enough that when roads are wet or icy, they are slippery.

These wet and slippery roads coupled with high speed will cause your vehicle to hydroplane. Hydroplaning is when traveling too fast, these conditions can result in losing control of the vehicle. You should slow down at least ten to fifteen miles per hour slower than the normal speed when these conditions exist. It is a very good idea not to use your brakes when the vehicle begins to slide. Shifting to a lower gear will most likely bring your vehicle to a slower, more controllable speed without the use of your brakes. This method may also be used in snowy or icy conditions. Braking suddenly can result in your vehicle sliding. If this should happen to you, releasing the brakes will most likely bring your vehicle back to its original position.

Always turn your steering wheel in the direction in which the rear of your car is sliding.

It does not matter how experienced you may think you are as a driver, respect for any kind of unusual road conditions proves you are a smart driver! Always respect the road conditions, wet or dry, especially during construction season. Respect the road workers by reducing your speed to the posted speed limit, and stay alert as you pass through these work zones.

HIGH WATER

You should never drive into fast moving water. It only takes approximately 18 inches of water to push the average automobile downstream. Approximately half of all flash flood fatalities are vehicle related.

In severe rainstorms, watch for high water and flooding at bridges and low areas. By venturing into this high water situation, you are placing yourself and others in extreme danger. Simply turn around and find an alternate route.

High wind can also affect your ability to control your vehicle. You should also slowdown in wind storms.

NIGHT DRIVING

Night driving has always been considered more dangerous because of lessened visibility. Your vision is usually limited to the maximum distance of your high-beam head lights. Normally this is about three to four hundred feet. It takes less than 5 seconds to absorb that distance driving at sixty miles per hour.

We should slow down five to fifteen miles per hour slower when driving at night, and even more if weather conditions are less than favorable. **Remember: Always dim your lights when following a vehicle or meeting oncoming traffic.**

WINTER DRIVING

In colder months, we have to deal with a different set of weather circumstances. Frozen precipitation, whether it be frost, sleet, or snow can not only accumulate on road surfaces making them treacherous to travel, it can accumulate on the windows of the automobile and this can obstruct your view from within and prevent you from having a clear view of the entire perimeter of the vehicle.

"Peep Hole" cleaning of your windshield and windows is not a proper way to clean away frost or snow.

The "Peep Hole," as it is referred to, does not reveal a clear and safe view for driving. Always remember: Completely clear all ice and snow from your windshield, windows and mirrors before driving. Too often one will clean just enough space to be able to see part of the roadway ahead. Not only is it dangerous, it is unlawful.

To venture out in icy or snowy conditions is taking an unnecessary risk to your safety. Then it challenges you're driving skill. We are usually warned in advance of bad weather conditions giving the average person time to adjust any necessary travel arrangements.

You may also find: When we have been warned to stay off the road in these conditions and there is a collision, your automobile insurance may not be supporting.

DRIVING IN FOG, SNOW, OR SMOKE

Try to avoid driving in a blinding snow storm. We are usually warned of bad weather conditions in advance so venture out only in emergency situations. Fog in some areas can be much denser than in "normal" fog conditions. We often see fog warning signs on the roadway that tell us of some of these areas; however, dense fog may occur most anywhere.

Always slowdown in foggy conditions, especially in night fog: **Keep your head lights on low beam for better vision. The same applies for smoky areas. Never drive into dense snow, fog, or smoke.**

If you should find yourself in dense fog, smoke or snow and your vision is limited to the point of near zero, try not to panic and stop your vehicle in the travel lane of the highway.

This action could lead to a disaster. Stopping in a travel lane any time other than when directed to do so by a safety officer could lead to a multi-vehicle pile-up. If you must stop in these limited vision conditions, it may be safer if you pull your vehicle to the right shoulder as far from the travel lane as it is safe for you to do so. If you can see the center line or right shoulder solid line, it may be safer for you to keep moving with your four way flashers activated.

CURVY ROADS

 Curvy roads are where many crashes occur. Always drive at a speed that is suitable to the road conditions and whereby you are able to stop your vehicle within a short and safe distance.

Slow down when approaching a curve. A safe speed is usually posted along with the familiar **"CURVY ROAD AHEAD"** sign. If the road is not visible 400 feet ahead of you, for safety your speed should not exceed 50 MPH. If the road is not clearly visible less than 400 feet, your speed should be reduced accordingly. Your velocity of speed and weight of your vehicle can prevent you from following the curvy conditions in a safe manner. Notice the guardrail if one is in place. The damage on these guardrails may show you how many drivers have failed to respect the curvy road conditions.

 More automobile crashes happen on straight roads rather than in curvy ones. In curvy conditions, a driver is usually more alert because of the road conditions.

On straight roadways too often a driver can easily become too relaxed and have a tendency to pay less attention to speed and their driving responsibilities.

A driver should enter a curve slow enough to allow them to slightly accelerate when rounding out the curve. **Entering a curve with speed too great for the road condition can cause one to be unable to control the vehicle.** Applying too much speed in curves may cause a person to pull across the center line and find themselves in the path of oncoming traffic. One may also drift too wide onto the shoulder which is almost certain danger.

Extra caution should be used in curvy road conditions when driving a top-heavy vehicle. **A pickup truck with a "Truck-Bed Camper" is an example of a top-heavy vehicle. If you can look straight over the top of your vehicle it would not be considered top-heavy; however, if you are of average height and cannot lay your hand flat on the top of your vehicle while standing flat footed, your vehicle could be top-heavy.** With this extra height your vehicle may be more difficult to handle in curvy roads, high wind conditions and when over correcting the steering wheel. This type of vehicle has a higher center-of-gravity and will handle completely different from a normal vehicle. The height and weight may cause one to misjudge their speed versus the radius of a curve which could cause the vehicle to turn over.

Many collisions can be prevented if a driver will stay alert when driving in curvy roads, toping a hill or passing through intersections. In curvy road crashes, inexperienced drivers and speed is often the cause of the crash.

CARBON MONOXIDE

Carbon monoxide (CO) is a colorless, odorless and poisonous gas produced by incomplete combustion of organic matter. Carbon monoxide may be produced in lethal quantities in automobile exhaust, faulty home heating systems, improperly used portable gas stoves and heaters, improperly vented wood stoves and fireplaces, and in many industrial situations.

One of the hazards of driving is carbon monoxide. The most common cause of this danger is a faulty exhaust system. In older vehicles, worn spots may appear in the floor board under the carpet or mat. This condition is commonly caused by rust. If your exhaust has a leak, this will place you and your passengers in extreme danger. If you are driving or riding in a vehicle and you feel dizziness or nauseated, roll your windows down as fresh air will likely cure the problem. **Remember: Carbon monoxide fumes are odorless and very deadly.**

NARROW BRIDGE

College Street 36266

Narrow Bridge signs are usually placed before the bridge to give drivers notice that they are about to drive over a narrow bridge. Narrow bridge signs are normally yellow with black text. **When you are approaching one of these bridges, slow down to avoid meeting any large vehicle such as a truck or bus. However, there is usually room for two cars to pass safely without incident.**

DRAWBRIDGE SIGNS AND SIGNALS

Drawbridges are mechanical bridges which are placed over navigable waters that rise or turn to allow marine traffic to go around or under them. When they begin to move, the roadway is closed to all traffic. Always use caution when driving or walking over a drawbridge. Do not move forward until the gates are raised and the lights stop flashing.

Modern day drawbridge in Florida

Many drawbridges have gates with flashing red lights and ringing bells. Stop when you see these lights begin to flash and before the gate lowers across your road lane. It is against the law to drive around or under a crossing gate, either down or being opened or closed. These drawbridge traffic lights should be treated just like a regular traffic control signal.

Flashing Yellow Light Signal--This is the first sign you will see when approaching a drawbridge. This light advises you to slow down and look for the DRAWBRIDGE SIGNAL. If the yellow light is flashing to indicate the drawbridge is in operation and the DRAWBRIDGE SIGNAL is red, prepare to stop.

RED: Come to a complete stop at the marked stop line. The bridge is in operation and roadway is closed to all pedestrian and motor vehicle traffic.

YELLOW: Stop if you can safely do so. The bridge is just about to start operation. If you are not able to stop, continue with caution and watch for the traffic gates.

VALUABLE DRIVING TIPS

GREEN: Go – watch out for pedestrians and other vehicles on the bridge.

CONTRA-FLOW OR REVERSIBLE LANES

Reversible lanes are also commonly found in tunnels and on bridges, and on the surrounding roadways — even where the lanes aren't regularly reversed to handle normal changes in traffic flow.

Contra-flow lane reversal is used to refer to plans that alter the normal flow of traffic, typically on a controlled access highway such as a freeway or motorway.

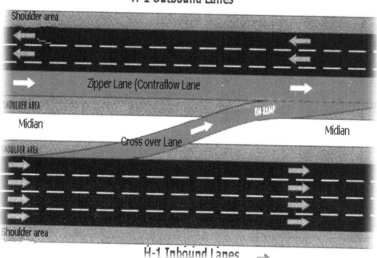

This is used to either aid in an emergency evacuation (the most common usage of the term in the United States) or, as part of routine maintenance activities such as to facilitate widening or reconstruction of the group of lanes on one side of the highway.

Usually, the term is used to refer to reversal of lanes which are normally only configured for travel in one direction; changing the configuration of reversible lanes, such as for rush hour, is not normally considered Contra-flow lane reversal.

PART SIX

THE MANUAL TRANSMISSION

We've all seen them on the road, bucking and stalling while learning how to drive a vehicle with what is called a "stick-shift". Knowing how to drive a vehicle before tackling the art of operating a manual transmission is highly recommended, but not required. Having to worry about shifting gears and what your left foot is doing is distracting enough; however, being uncomfortable behind the wheel, no matter what transmission the car has, makes it even worse. The area where you first practice should be flat, free of obstructions and obviously have no vehicular or pedestrian traffic.

When seated in the vehicle make sure you are sitting close enough to push the clutch, the leftmost pedal, all the way to the floor. The gear shift should be within easy reach as well. Take time to familiarize yourself with the shift pattern before you need to keep your eyes on the road.

Once you are in a comfortable seating position and are familiar with the location of the clutch and shift pattern, double-check to make sure the parking brake (lever just to the right of the driver's seat) is set and put the car into neutral by pushing down the clutch and putting the stick into neutral. You will be able to move the gearshift back and forth through its whole horizontal movement while you are in neutral.

Push the clutch to the floor again, and start the vehicle. Even though the engine will run in neutral, modern vehicles have a lockout system disabling the ability to start the vehicle unless the clutch is fully depressed. Once the vehicle is started, let the clutch up slowly, just to make sure the vehicle really isn't in gear.

If a person is first learning to drive a vehicle with a manual transmission he or she will have a tendency to cause the vehicle to jump and jerk when trying to go forward. To prevent the jerking of the vehicle you should ease out on the clutch as you lightly accelerate. If the jerking continues, push the clutch in and repeat the process applying a slight more acceleration. The vehicle should go forward smoothly.

Accelerate to approximately 10 mph, push the clutch to the floor releasing your acceleration and pull the gear selector down to the second gear position. Let the clutch out and raise the speed to approximately 20 mph. Repeat the same pattern and push the selector to the third gear position. By the time you have reached 40 mph, you should be in the fourth gear. If your vehicle has a 5-gear transmission your last gear position should be completed by 45 to 50 mph.

It takes the same gears to stop as it takes to start moving. As you decrease your speed you should apply the clutch and push your selector into the third gear position. Repeat the same process until you are at about 10 mph. At this point you should be in your first gear. As the speed falls to 5 mph, you should push your clutch in, preparing to stop.

You should not push your clutch in at a cruising speed and leave it in all the way to your stop, nor should you drive with your foot resting on the clutch pedal.

CRUISE CONTROL

Auto cruise is a great convenience. However, it should not be used in hilly country or curvy road conditions, or in city freeway driving. **The cruise control is more effective in areas where the highway is straighter, such as in four lane highways or express ways where it is less likely to have stop signs or stop lights.**

One should always avoid using cruise control in any heavy traffic even though the traffic may be moving smoothly.

These areas are not compatible for the use of cruise control. Cruise control should not be engaged when weather conditions are less than favorable, such as on wet highways or in snowy or icy conditions. Hydroplaning could occur, resulting in the loss of control of your vehicle. **Inexperienced drivers should not use**

cruise control. Learn to maintain a steady speed without using cruise control.

CONTROLLING AN OVER ACCELERATED ENGINE

In a time when a spring and a metal rod controlled the acceleration, a spring could break off or slip off leaving the driver without accelerator control. Often times when this would happen, the acceleration would just die. However, it could go the opposite way and cause the accelerator to drop to the floor, leading the driver into a state of confusion as how to handle the situation. Fortunately, back in the days of the manual transmission, the person who assisted in teaching someone to drive always explained the following: if this should happen while you are driving, simply push the clutch in and put the transmission into the neutral position because a vehicle only has force power while it is in gear.

Today, the accelerator is controlled by a different method; air and or electronics. However, the same results exist. If you should experience an out of control acceleration, simply push the gear selector to the neutral position. Although your engine's RPM may remain at the high speed, you will get yourself out of speeding danger. Pushing the gear to reverse or the park position only destroys the transmission. **Remember: your vehicle has no power in neutral.**

It would not be advisable to turn the ignition switch off while the vehicle is in motion in this type of emergency because the steering may become locked limiting your ability to stay in control of your speeding vehicle. Using your neutral gear will allow you to apply soft braking and in normal conditions you will be able to bring the vehicle under control without damage. Knowing how to use your emergency brake can also help correct this condition.

OVER CORRECTING THE STEERING WHEEL

Over correcting is a major cause of automobile crashes. If your vehicle, for any reason, should drop off the shoulder of the highway, you should never pull it back onto the road too quickly. In most cases, you should allow the vehicle to travel a short distance and then ease it back onto the roadway. Grasp the steering wheel firmly with both hands and ease the vehicle back in position without a quick pulling of the steering wheel. A sudden jerking action will most likely cause the driver to lose control of the vehicle. This sometimes occurs when one is attempting to miss an object or an animal. In most cases it would be more logical to hit a small animal rather than to try and get out of its way.

Many crashes have accrued, some fatal when the driver swerves to miss a wild animal.

You should never hit your brakes, or pull on the steering wheel, this action will most always be a bad choice. You may use your brakes only if the vehicle is moving straight.

Over correcting may be caused by a number of things. Your vehicle may be moving in a straight manner down the highway and a sudden jerk of the steering wheel could cause the vehicle to swerve and roll over and never leave the pavement. The velocity of speed; and the weight can cause you to be unable to stay in control.

UNSAFE TIRES

Some automobile collisions are caused by equipment failure; and, most often this is because of a blown out tire. Always be cautious of running tires that may be too worn for safe driving.

Slick tires can blow out, which could cause you to lose control of your vehicle. Tires which are too slick can also be extremely dangerous in wet or icy weather conditions. A small stone or any small object in the roadway which may not even be noticeable can puncture thin tires and cause them to blow out.

If a tire should blow out while you are driving, allow the vehicle to slow down, mostly on its own, by only applying soft braking. Shifting to a lower gear will also help to slow down your vehicle. Never apply hard brakes as this may cause the vehicle to begin a skid or turn over.

If you do not know how to judge the condition of your tires, you may choose to use the copper penny method for measuring the tread. Take a penny, hold it at the base of Lincoln's head and insert the top of Lincoln's head in between the tread of the tire. If all of Lincoln's head can be seen, your tire is unsafe for driving. If half the head can be seen, you are in a cautious zone and should begin to think about getting new tires. Tires which are too worn are illegal on the roadways.

Tires should be inflated to the vehicle manufacturer's recommended pressure printed on the vehicle's door placard, or in the owner's manual. It should not be inflated to the maximum limit on the tire side wall.

Under inflated tires can flex too much and build up heat which can lead to a blowout of the tire. Under inflated tires will cause the vehicle to pull slightly to the side of the slack tire. Rear slack tires can cause the vehicle to sway which may affect your steering control.

KNOW HOW TO USE YOUR EMERGENCY BRAKES

One very important and potentially lifesaving device most drivers probably never use on their automobile is their emergency brake. It is **NEVER** talked about in most driver training programs or on driving tests!

I personally knew someone who died in a simple collision that could have been prevented had she known how to use her emergency brake.

The other fatal mistake made in this same collision was that the driver panicked and turned off the ignition switch. In most vehicles this locks the steering wheel and prevents you from safely maneuvering your vehicle.

Go to a large deserted parking lot or an empty remote back road and practice stopping with your emergency brake. Most drivers think the automobile automatically comes to a screeching halt if you use the emergency brake. This is not the case at all if you apply steady and constant pressure on the handle or pedal until you come to a complete stop.

BRAKES AND THE ANTI-LOCKING BRAKE SYSTEM

When you apply your brakes and there is a grinding or squeaking sound, your brakes are most likely worn out. Have them checked as soon as possible. Do not continue to drive as these sounds mean your braking power is dangerously reduced.

Most vehicles are equipped with what is called the anti-lock brake system or ABS. **ABS is a safety system which prevents the wheels on a motor vehicle from locking up (or ceasing to rotate) while braking.** This electronic system prevents the wheels from locking when the brakes are applied forcefully. Using sensors, a control unit determines if the wheels are starting to lock and brake pressure is then reduced. This advanced technology is designed to prevent brakes from locking up regardless of brake pedal pressure. Anti-lock braking systems have become increasingly popular because they enhance traction in slippery conditions and allow you to keep steering control of a vehicle, even in a skid. ABS is a computer-controlled system that can "sense", in a braking situation, when one or more wheels have stopped turning; yet the vehicle is still moving. The computer will then quickly release and re-apply the brakes repeatedly thus giving the driver more control of the vehicle.

If your vehicle has the ABS braking system you should brake as you always have. Use only the breaking force necessary to stop safely and stay in control. If someone suddenly pulls out in front of you, your natural response is to hit your brakes. This action is good if there is enough space to stop and stay in control of your vehicle. Hard breaking and releasing brakes will sometimes help to keep your vehicle straight and avoid skidding uncontrollably.

One of the most important benefits of ABS is that the driver can steer the vehicle away from hazards while braking. Drivers should not turn the steering wheel hard or jerk the vehicle in one direction. Control of the vehicle can be maintained by steering where the driver wants to go. Drivers need to check to make sure traffic is clear when deciding where to steer and always remember to steer back into the original lane as soon as the hazard is cleared.

Drivers can determine whether their cars have ABS by looking for a lighted ABS symbol on the dashboard right after starting the engine, checking the owner's manual or asking the dealer.

MIRRORS

Your mirrors are your eyes behind you. A responsible driver will glance in the rearview mirror about every thirty to forty-five seconds. It is very important to be aware of any vehicle approaching from the rear.

Drivers who do not monitor their mirrors may not notice a vehicle even when it is in plain view. When you are about to pass, assume the driver you are about to pass does not see you, they could suddenly move in front of you without even realizing your there. Always be sure the lane is clear before moving to the next lane.

Adjust the inside mirror so that it frames the entire rearview window. It is the primary mirror for monitoring what is behind your vehicle. Your side mirror should be adjusted to reduce the blind spots. Each side mirror should be adjusted so the driver can barely see the side of the vehicle on either side. This will allow a better view of the road beside and behind you.

You should never pile objects on the rear deck behind the back seat. This will limit the ability to get the full view through your rear window. Also, you should not rely on your mirrors for backing up. Your mirrors may not be your best view for changing lanes. Check both rearview as well as your side mirrors.

When passing another vehicle, never rely on your right side mirror to show you the accurate clear distance of your vehicle and the vehicle you have just passed. The right side mirror does not normally reveal the true image.

WIPER BLADES

Worn out wiper blades cause streaking in rainy conditions which cause poor visibility. Changing them when they become worn will increase safety and give better visibility. **When wiper blades become worn they can cause permanent damage to your windshield.** They can lean to the side causing the metal brackets which hold the blades in place to touch the windshield. This contact will scratch the glass causing permanent damage.

HEADLIGHTS

Your headlights should be turned on when your vehicle is not visible to others within 500 feet. If the weather is clear, your lights should be turned on when the sun stops casting a shadow.

On cloudy days, your lights should be turned on earlier than on clear days. This suggestion should apply to early mornings as well. **It's not a matter of how well you can see, it's how well others are able to see you.**

In rain, fog, smoke, or snowy weather you should always drive with your headlights on for safety reasons. This will allow any oncoming traffic to see you more clearly. Always use your low beams as not to cast an unnecessary reflection from the highway on the oncoming traffic. **When driving behind any vehicle at night you should use your low beams so as not to blind the driver in the vehicle ahead of you with the reflection in the mirrors.**

When driving at night, do not look directly at the headlights of an oncoming vehicle. Direct your eyes to the right edge of the highway and try to look beyond the glare of the headlights.

You should check all the lights on your vehicle often to be sure head lights, taillights, tag lights, and signal lights are all in proper working condition.

One of the leading causes of automobiles being pulled over by law enforcement officers is faulty lights, failing to dim your lights, and failing to give proper signals.

THE SIGNAL IS ON, BUT NO ONE IS TURNING

You should always be cautious of crossing any intersection while giving a turning signal, even if your turn is close to, but past, the intersection. Your signal could send a wrong message to someone who may be waiting to enter the highway, or to an oncoming vehicle waiting to turn across your lane. After you have made the turn, you should make a habit of glancing at your dash board instrument panel to see if you have left your turn signals on. It is a good habit to look at your instrument panel often. This will help you be aware of the speed you are traveling so you can make the appropriate adjustments. It will also keep you informed of your water temperature, or oil pressure level.

 When you are following a vehicle which is attempting to turn or is stopping, you should give the same signal as the vehicle in front of you so as to alert the vehicles behind you of the situation.

Many times your vehicle may be blocking the view of the cars behind you and preventing them from realizing the stop or turn is being initiated. This lack of signal could lead to an automobile collision. **Also, when you are giving a signal to stop or make a turn, glance in your rearview mirror to be sure the vehicle behind you has recognized your signal. This action can prevent a rear end collision.**

When planning to make a turn, you should turn your signal on before you apply your brakes in preparation to slow down. This will allow anyone behind you to be better prepared for the pending situation ahead.

If you are following a vehicle and the driver is frequently hitting his brakes, this action indicates a nervous or insecure driver. If you can't pass and move out of their zone, then increase the distance between you and the vehicle in front of you and follow with caution.

WARNING LIGHTS

 If you should see a red warning light on your dash board come on while you are driving, this is an

indication your engine may be running hot and your oil or water may be dangerously low. Find a convenient place to pull over as soon as possible.

If the warning light is indicating an overheated engine because of low water, never try to remove the radiator cap immediately. Extreme pressure may have built up from the overheated engine and this could place you in danger of being badly burned. Most radiators have a separate reservoir for adding water. High pressure does not normally build up in this overflow container. However, always use caution.

If you should find the reservoir empty, you should refill it while the engine is running. Under normal low-water circumstances this will usually allow you to drive on a few miles until the system can be checked for leaks. However, never run your vehicle when it is overheating. This could cause extensive damage to your engine.

If the indicator light has come on because of low oil pressure, you should turn the switch off and not restart the engine until the oil level has been checked and, if necessary, oil has been added and you have checked for any severe oil leaks. If you continue to drive when either of the red indicator lights are on you will put the engine in danger of locking up. You should keep your critical driving components like water, oil, tires, lights, and wiper blades checked often. Your safety and the safety of others depend on these components.

If your vehicle engine should stop running and you have pulled over to check for the problem, never use a raw flame to help light up a dark area; use only a battery powered light. **A raw flame can ignite vapors which may be unnoticed to the eyes or nose.**

HORNS

How often do you use your car horn? How often should we use them? Are there standards of etiquette that everyone should observe? **Valid messages to communicate with the horn: "There's about to be a collision if we don't take action." "My car is malfunctioning and is not in my control." "The light is green now.** If we honk to get their attention, it should be a quick beep, not a long blast.

The horn should only be used to alert danger. To signal a friend with the horn is annoying to other motorists. Use only when appropriate!

PART SEVEN

SHARING THE ROAD

The vehicle in front of you usually has the right of way. However, not every driver seems to know this. For example, let's say you are traveling in the right lane on a four-lane highway when you notice the vehicle in front of you has turned on his left turn signal. Usually, this signal indicates that the vehicle in front of you is approaching a slower moving vehicle and, in order to maintain a steady speed, it has become necessary for the driver in front of you to change lanes. However, 80% of those following that vehicle think the signal means for them to quickly change lanes, accelerate, and pass both the signaling vehicle and the slower moving vehicle. This action not only hinders the signaling vehicle from completing the pass, it is very dangerous and inconsiderate. Most commercial equipment operators will tell you this happens to them many times every day. This action shows a total lack of respect for any driver, whether it is heavy equipment, or an automobile. **Legally and respectfully, the vehicle in front of you has the right to, and should be allowed to take, the first**

opportunity to pass. This is why it's called the "Right Of Way."

PICKUP TRUCKS

The pickup truck is a fun vehicle for many teenagers. However, we must always be cautious of carrying passengers in the back cargo area of the truck. Some state laws prohibit riding in the back of the truck, or may have an age limit on those who may ride there. **Always be sure these passengers are seated on the floor of the truck bed, and never allow passengers to stand up or sit on the side body while the vehicle is in motion. (Refer to tips for all p.158 tips 16)**

SHARING THE ROAD WITH TWO WHEELERS

Motorcycles have the same rights and responsibilities on the public highways as any other highway user. As a former bike rider, I have seen plenty of instances of general motorists not respecting the rights of the rider. When there is a collision involving a motorcycle the response most often given by the automobile driver will be, "I didn't see him coming."

Following too closely to a cycle rider could cause the rider to become nervous and he or she could become distracted from the road ahead. Also, be careful not to brake too fast if a motorcycle is following you too closely.

There were 4,595 fatal crashes involving motorcycles across the United States in 2009. In those crashes, more than 84,000 were injured.

 Many automobile collisions involving a motorcycle happen during a left turn attempt. Automobile drivers should never drive in the same lane alongside a motorcycle even if one thinks there is plenty of room.

This action is illegal and is most dangerous. You should also use the same following distance behind a motorcycle as you would any other vehicle.

Traffic laws also apply to bicycle riders as well. However, many children are unaware of these laws. Therefore, the adult rider should not only teach children the rules of the road, but should also set a good example by obeying the riding laws.

Every bicycle rider should ride as closely to the right curb or shoulder as comfortably possible. The rider should also wear a colorful helmet and reflective clothing so as to be seen more clearly by passing motorist.

SHARING THE ROAD WITH LARGE VEHICLES AND WIDE LOADS

 "WIDE LOAD" means a vehicle is wider than usual, or it is carrying a load that is wider than the truck itself.

Always yield to any wide load vehicle. We must always remember a loaded truck or any large vehicle cannot stop as quickly as a pickup truck or a car. **Many times that large vehicle coming toward you can weigh more than fifty tons!** That is almost like a train coming directly toward you. Here is one scenario that often results in an automobile collision and this situation could be on the expressway, in stop and go traffic or in a traffic-light-controlled area.

For example: You may notice a space between large vehicles, possibly an 18-wheeler or bus, and the vehicle in front of them. This space is the stopping distance they fix for a safety cushion. **This cushion distance is very important in order to keep them from running into the rear end of the vehicle they are following.**

You will notice impatient automobile drivers are constantly darting into that space just to gain an extra few feet in the flow of traffic. This unconcerned action reduces the stopping distance of the large vehicle by 30 or more feet. If the braking power has already been exhausted by the large vehicle, there could be an unavoidable rear end collision.

 Don't put yourself in the path of an oncoming collision. Avoid creating a condition whereby you could be at fault. Again, the best highway safety insurance you can

have is the space you keep between you and the vehicle in front of you.

Dangerous driving zones are the areas around other cars, trucks, and buses where your vehicle can disappear from the view of the other driver. "Blind spots" are where automobile collisions are most likely to happen. Always remember: if you can't see the mirror of the truck or bus in front of you, the driver cannot see you.

We are told that every 15 minutes an eighteen wheeler is involved in a collision with an automobile. Therefore, give that space and a little extra time. It could be the wisest and safest thing you will ever do. Never "hang out" on either side of these large vehicles.

If you are beside a vehicle and find that you are both going the same speed, speed up or slow down and merge in front or behind the other vehicle. Too often a heavy equipment driver will be upon us before we realize he is coming. In this case, simply speed up so you can see a lane clearly on either side and move over to get out of the dangerous path.

When passing large vehicles, such as buses or trucks, do not cut back in too quickly. Wait until you can see the entire front end of the vehicle in your rear view mirror, not the right side mirror, before pulling back in the desired lane; then, move on out of their way as not to hinder their speed.

Driving too closely behind another vehicle is known as "Tailgating" and it is very dangerous. You must realize that a large vehicle operator cannot see you clearly if you are closer than 200 feet.

If you are driving too closely behind a large vehicle and it suddenly becomes necessary for them to brake, you could find yourself plowing into the rear end of the stopping vehicle, becoming a victim of your own negligence.

Never walk or drive behind a large vehicle which is attempting to back up. Their vision behind the vehicle is limited to what they can see in the mirrors. In most cases the driver may be unable to see you at all.

You should never pull out in front of any vehicle if it is going to cause that vehicle to have to slow down because of your

actions. For example, if you pull up to a stop sign intersection and you see a vehicle about 500 feet away coming in your direction traveling at a speed of 60 Mph or greater and you feel the need to pull out in front of that vehicle, it would be necessary for your vehicle to accelerate to 65 mph within the first quarter of a mile in order to keep that vehicle from having to slow down because of your action.

If that oncoming vehicle is an eighteen-wheeler or motor coach, you are placing yourself and others in extreme danger by pulling out at a low speed. If you are crossing the intersection under the same circumstances, you may be able to clear the intersection before that oncoming vehicle gets to you, if your vehicle doesn't stall. On the other hand, if we will just wait about 4 seconds that approaching vehicle will have passed. Safety first and patience will pay off!

THE SQUEEZE IN

Large vehicle, such as an eighteen wheeler, sometimes need to have extra room when they are making a right turn. When a large vehicle is attempting to make a right turn, it is sometimes necessary for the driver to swing wide to the left before making the turn, and often times they will need two lanes to make the right turn.

Always watch to see if the turn signal is on and avoid passing at this point.

Allow a short time for the driver to complete his turn to avoid the squeezed-in danger. Give them the space necessary to carry their load more safely on the highways and through the intersection.

THREE-LANE HIGHWAYS

In some areas of the country, mostly on secondary roads, we still find places where a passing lane has been built for the purpose of passing slower moving vehicles. This allows vehicles to maintain a more steady speed in hilly country or congested areas. Even though your state law may not advise "Drive to the Right", you should always do this for safety and courtesy reasons. **When you pass a slower moving vehicle in one of these passing zones, you should pull back into the right lane soon as possible because the middle lane can also be used for passing from the other direction as indicated in the picture. Keeping to the right at night may be more important because it may be more difficult for the oncoming traffic to realize which lane you are traveling in. Keeping to the right could prevent a head-on collision.**

CENTER TURN LANES

Center turn lanes are designed for left turning traffic only. These lanes should not be used for passing.

A two-way, left-turn lane is a lane in the center of a highway or city street that is set aside for use by vehicles making left turns in either direction. Use caution and stay alert when in the center turn lane. Yield to the oncoming traffic.

PASSING ZONE

When passing on a two lane highway, you should not pass more than two vehicles at a time.

Passing is not allowed on hills, curves, intersections, bridges or railroad crossings. Passing is also illegal anywhere the double yellow line is present or when the solid yellow line is to the right of the dashed center line.

If you are following a vehicle on a two lane highway and do not intend to pass, you should keep enough space between you and the vehicle you are following in case another vehicle needs to pass. This space will help avoid the need for double passing.

Passing is <u>only</u> allowed when there is a single, dashed center line, or when there is a dashed center line to the right of a solid yellow line. These are known as safe passing zones.

The opportunity to pass a vehicle seems to be a very important thing to many young drivers. This action also applies to the older drivers as well. Some just can't seem to be comfortable with the idea of following someone. They feel they must be out in front, and many times they will pass when there is not enough clear road space in the front of the vehicle they are trying to pass. **Passing should be done only when conditions demand that you do so.**

If you feel that using the passing gear is necessary for you to pass, you probably do not have time to pass and be safe in doing so. **You should not use the passing gear until you are pulled out to the next lane and are clear of the vehicle you are passing.**

There have been some occasions where using the passing gear to quickly, before pulling out to the next lane has resulted in hitting the vehicle one was attempting to pass. Other occasions have resulted in a spin-out and total loss of vehicle control.

When passing a vehicle, you should move on out of the way as swiftly and safely as possible. This practice should be exercised whether you are on a two lane highway or an expressway.

Never pass and then slowdown in front of the vehicle you have just passed. Know the size of your vehicle and learn where your correct placement position is within your travel lane. Driving too close to the center line is dangerous. Be aware of keeping your vehicle the correct distance between the center line and the shoulder. Like the old saying goes, "Keep it between the lines !"

Many highway deaths and serious injuries happen on two-lane highways when vehicles collide head-on or side swipe each other.

Lack of driving experience, improper passing and inter-car activities contribute to most all of these types of vehicle crashes. **Distractions remain one of the greatest causes of automobile collisions.**

CROSSROADS AND INTERSECTIONS

A crossroad is typically where two roads cross each other. Sometimes, you may find a four-way stop, or one direction may have to stop or yield the right of way while the other direction may keep moving. Usually you are warned three to five hundred feet in advance of the junction. If stopping is required, be sure the right of way is clear before proceeding. At a four or three way stop normally, the person to your right has the right of way. Or, one may consider the person who arrives at the stop sign first as having the right of way.

Drivers who do not understand the rules pertaining to who has the right-of-way at intersections are a major cause of automobile collisions. These rules may differ depending on the configuration of the intersection, such as a one way street, or, merging into another street or highway. Study and understand the right-of-way laws!

One very dangerous scenario is when you come to an intersection and will be making a right turn. Let's say, you come to a stop sign at a 2-lane highway. Most of the time a driver will look to the left and, if the way is clear, proceed to make the right turn. This can turn deadly if there was a vehicle approaching from your right which is in the process of passing another vehicle, when you execute your right turn you are face-to-face with the vehicle that is in your lane! Always look both ways before proceeding.

When two common vehicles come to an uncontrolled intersection or a four-way stop at the same time, the vehicle on your right should be given the first right of way. At a three-way stop the same rule applies so use common courtesy.

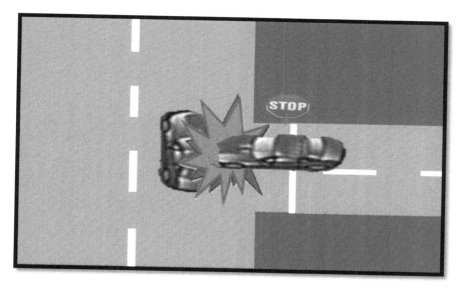

When an intersection is controlled by traffic lights and when this light has stopped working, we should approach with caution and treat the intersection as a four way stop. REMEMBER: Always look left, look right, and then look left again!

Remember: At any intersection where you are required to stop, wait until the way is clear, and then proceed with caution. In almost every circumstance, waiting 10 seconds will most likely clear the right-of-way.

Vehicles entering stop or yield intersections. The right-of-way at an intersection may be indicated by stop signs or yield signs, except when directed to proceed by a police officer or traffic control signal. Every driver of a vehicle approaching a stop intersection, indicated by a stop sign, must stop at a clearly marked stop line. However, if none, stop before entering the crosswalk on the near side of the intersection. If there is no crosswalk then stop at the point nearest the intersecting roadway where the driver has a view of approaching traffic. After having stopped, the driver shall yield the right-of-way to any vehicle which has entered the intersection from another highway or which is approaching so closely on said highway as to constitute an immediate hazard during the time when the driver is moving across or within the intersection.

At a four-way stop intersection, the driver of the first vehicle to stop at the intersection shall be the first to proceed. If two or more vehicles reach the four-way stop intersection at the same time, the driver of the vehicle on the left shall yield the right-of-way to the vehicle on the right.

The driver of a vehicle approaching a yield sign shall, in obedience to such sign, slow down to a speed reasonable for the existing conditions and, if required for safety to stop, shall stop before entering the crosswalk on the near side of the intersection.

If such a driver is involved in a collision with a pedestrian in a crosswalk or a vehicle in the intersection, after driving past a yield sign without stopping, the collision shall be deemed prima facie evidence of the driver's failure to yield the right-of-way. **A violation of this section is a noncriminal traffic infraction, punishable as a moving violation.**

PART EIGHT

TURNS AND HAND SIGNALS

In some turning situations, you may choose to use your hand signal. Depending on the lighting at the time, or the vantage point of the driver to whom you are signaling, your hand signal may be more visible than a turn signal.

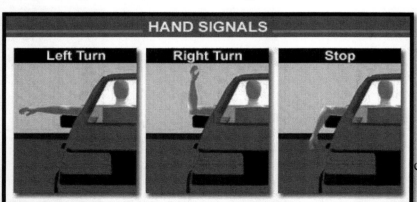

cess

In many heavy traffic intersections, a green arrow may allow you to turn while opposing traffic is stopped. Always use caution when turning as some drivers may not be paying attention to the signals.

Some turn lanes are marked with overhead signs, and some are marked on the pavement. There are single turn lanes and double turn lanes. Go slow and keep your vehicle within the proper lane to complete your turn.Prepare for the turn before you get to it. **Never make a last minute decision to turn if you recognize your turn too late and cannot complete it safely. Look for a suitable place to turn around, and then go back to your turn.** Move into the proper turn lane well in advance, 100 feet or more if possible, and be sure it is safe to make the turn. Follow through with your turn and maintain the proper lane.

Traffic turning left should always yield to the oncoming traffic. **We must look to make sure we know the approximate speed of an oncoming vehicle before making that left turn.** Learning how to judge distance is important. You do this by observing before turning. Again, a 10-second wait will give you time to assess the situation. When turning left, you may be in a marked turn lane or just turning from a two lane highway. If there are more than one vehicle turning, you must always wait until the vehicle in front of you has clearly left the turning lane before you proceed.

 Many collisions happen when one is attempting to make a left turn. Always look, and look again, before making that left turn at busy intersections.

Turning a corner too short could cause your vehicle to come in contact with an object such as a high curb or you could even drop off the shoulder of the driveway.

RUSH HOUR LANES

A **Rush Hour** or **Peak Hour** is a part of the day during which traffic congestion on roads and crowding on public transport is the worst. Normally, this happens twice a day — once in the morning and once in the evening; the times during which most people commute to/from work and school.

Some roads in larger cities will have reversible lanes. These lanes are used to accommodate heavy traffic flows that change depending on the time of day.

RUSH HOUR CRASHES

Many are caused by lane hoppers who have less patients and feel they must suddenlly change lanes in order to gain a few feet in the flow of traffic.

Reversible lanes for rush hour traffic:

Morning Rush Hour Lane Configuration

Non-Rush-Hour Lane Configuration

Evening Rush Hour Lane Configuration

In the morning, you may have heavier traffic flow in one direction than another. In the evening, the heavier traffic flow is in the opposite direction. In between the rush hours, one lane may be used as a turn lane or not used at all.

PROPER TURNS AT MAJOR INTERSECTIONS

Study these diagrams and become familiar with the proper turn. Illustrations here show both two-way and one-way traffic turn patterns. Always look ahead and to each side of the intersection for other vehicles which may interfere with a safe turn.

Never cross a lane to make your turn. This action is known as a "lane violation". It's illegal and very unsafe.

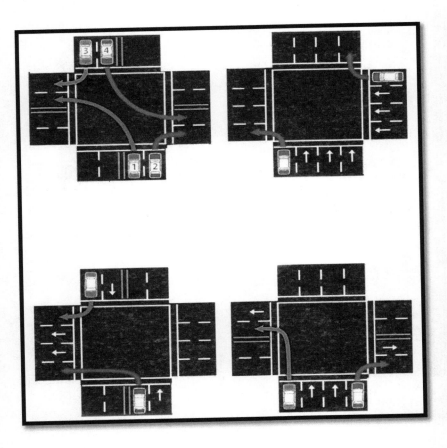

ONE SHOULD NOT CROSS AN INTERSECTION WITH THE TURN SIGNAL ACTIVATED, EVEN IF THE TURN IS NEAR BUT PASSED THE INTERSECTION. THE SIGNAL COULD SEND THE WRONG MESSAGE TO SOMEONE WAITING TO ENTER THE HIGHWAY, OR WAITING TO CROSS THE INTERSECTION.

THE ROUNDABOUT

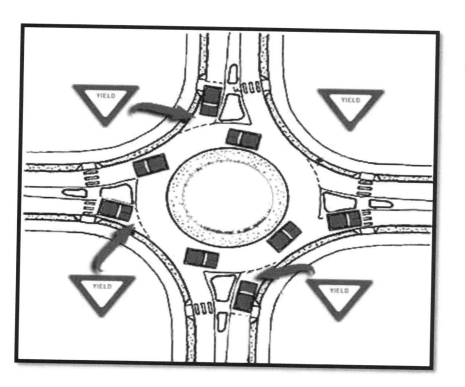

A "modern roundabout" is a type of circular junction that was developed by the UK's Transport Research Laboratory in the mid twentieth century, **in which road traffic must travel in one direction around a central island and priority is given to the circulating flow.** Signs usually direct traffic entering the circle to slow down and yield the right of way.

The vehicle inside the circle has the right of way. Normally, you will yield to the vehicle approaching from your left. As you enter, continue to move slowly with caution, through the circle to your desired exit.

THE THREE-POINT TURN

It doesn't have to be a hassle to get out of simple traffic binds. There are simple steps to mastering the three-point turn.

The official way to perform a three-point turn is to pull to the side of the road, turn wheels towards the center and accelerate until the car is a few feet from the opposite curb. Then turn the wheel in the opposite direction. Using reverse, back up until the vehicle's rear tires are close to the curb on the opposite side of the street and then turn the steering wheel again toward the center to position the wheels in the desired direction and accelerate forward in the new direction.

 The 3-Point turn is not permitted on freeways, hills, curves, near intersections or in heavy traffic. This action should only be done when your vehicle is visible to oncoming traffic for at least 500 feet.

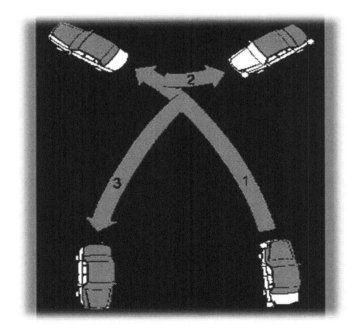

While teaching another, lead by example: Head to a low-traffic non-residential area and take the wheel. Show you're teen exactly how to perform the three-point turn and provide on-going commentary as to what you're doing. Point out the "crucial" areas of the turn such as proper initial positioning, turning the wheel completely before moving, and proper distance from curbs.

Use a stopwatch: No, it's not a race so have your teen time you to determine how long it takes to complete a three-point turn. This will be useful for determining a proper gap in traffic before starting the turn.

Get out of the car: Have your child get out of the car and watch the procedure from the road. Point out how the car is positioned close to the right side of the street before you begin the maneuver. Also point out how the car is perpendicular to the curb at the second "point". This will help him or her get a feel of where the car should be when they begin practicing.

These turns are usually governed by local ordinances and signs may not be posted to warn you. Prohibitory signs are usually posted in hazardous areas.

PARALLEL PARKING

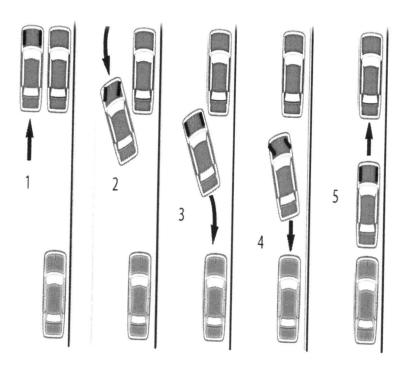

Here are some simple instructions to help you learn how to parallel park.

Seek out a space you feel comfortable that you can safely get your car into without crunching into another car.

Check your rearview mirror and driver-side mirror as you approach the space to ensure another car is not riding on your bumper. Signal toward the space as you approach it, slow down, and stop. If another motorist drives up to close to your vehicle, simply maintain your position and keep signaling. You might even need to roll down your window and wave the other driver around. They might not have realized you're trying to park.

Line up your vehicle with the parked vehicle directly in front of your desired spot. Don't get too close on the side or you might scrape the other car when you make your move. But, you also don't want to be too far away—two or three feet will suffice. Position your vehicle parallel to the parked car, aligning your bumpers or staying two or three feet behind.

Put your vehicle in reverse. Check the driver-side mirror to make sure the street behind you is clear of traffic before you begin to back up. Then look over your other shoulder at the space to assess the gap. Turn the steering wheel hard right. You are about to execute the first part of the five point turn.

Release the brakes and *slowly* begin backing into the turn. Visually check in front of and around your car often. Make sure you remain far enough away from the rear bumper of the vehicle in front of you as you slide in. If your rear tire hits the curb, you've gone too far; just shift gears and pull forward a few feet if this happens.

Turn the steering wheel to the left once the rear of your vehicle is predominantly in the space still going backward. This is the last half of the five point turn where you snake your way completely into the space and straighten out your car at the same time. Continue in reverse as far back as you can without tapping the bumper of the vehicle behind you.

Shift into drive, turn the steering wheel to the right again and move forward gently toward the curb while centering your vehicle in the space.

PARKING AND PRIVATE PARKING LOTS

When parking on a hill, you should make sure your car does not roll into the traffic if the brakes fail to hold. Shift to the park position if you have one. If not, shift to the low gear; and, if your vehicle is facing <u>downhill</u>, turn your wheels *toward* the adjacent curb. If your vehicle is facing <u>uphill</u> turn your wheels *away from* the adjacent curb.

When a vehicle is making an attempt to back out of a parking space, the oncoming vehicle should yield. **The approaching vehicle has a much better view than the vehicle which may be in reverse.** This person's view is limited to his mirrors or looking over his or he shoulder. The blind spot created by this position can block their otherwise clear view. If it is raining or there are other interfering weather conditions, this could also obstruct the backing view. If you don't have 5 seconds to wait, this may be a good time to sound the horn.

Parking areas such as parking garages or lots are usually private property. When in a private parking lot, you should respect and yield to the vehicle who is backing up.

These private property areas may create a problem if there is a collision. Your legal options may be limited.

Parking Lot Collision Law: Because most parking lot collisions occur on private property, insurance companies become the final arbiters in deciding who is at fault and who will pay for damage.

Under these circumstances, you will be responsible for getting the other party's information and testimonies from witnesses. This will be essential should you need to defend your case. Almost without exception, drivers will have very different perspectives of what took place, and under these circumstances the testimony of witnesses will be invaluable -- especially since the word of your passenger(s) will not be taken into account.

If you are unable to procure the other party's information, write down as much as you can get on your own (such as license plate numbers and witnesses' accounts). The usual reasons an individual will refuse to give you insurance information are that they do not have insurance or they believe you are at fault for the collision. This would leave you at fault. A result in no fault and in both instances you are liable. This would also indicate they do not want to file against their own insurance. However, this thought is misguided.

If you fail to file a claim, you might jeopardize your coverage. Attempt to call the police again, if necessary, to have them come to the scene so you can file a report. If they will not come to the scene because it took place on private property, go to the nearest police station and file a report. All this information can assist you when filing with the insurance company and in its determination of who is at fault.

CLICK-IT OR TICKET

A seat belt or seatbelt, sometimes called a safety belt, is a safety harness designed to secure the occupant of a vehicle against harmful movement that may result from a collision or a sudden stop.

As part of an overall automobile passive safety system, seat belts are intended to reduce injuries by stopping the wearer from hitting hard interior elements of the vehicle, or other passengers (the so-called second impact). Passengers are in the correct position for the airbag to deploy and prevent the passenger from being thrown from the vehicle. Seat belts also absorb energy by being designed to stretch during any sudden deceleration, so that there is less speed differential between the passenger's body and their vehicle interior, and also to spread out the loading of impact on the passenger's body.

One of the first questions asked when there is a collision is: "Were they wearing their seat belts". Seat belts are not the cause, nor are they normally the prevention of automobile crashes. The reason for safety belts is for your safety. In a crash you are far more likely to be killed if you are not wearing one.

Wearing shoulder belts and a lap belt make your chances of living through a crash twice as good.

In a crash, safety belts keep you from being thrown from the vehicle. Your risk of death is five times greater if you are thrown from the vehicle.

Safety belts keep you from being thrown against others in the vehicle and even against the steering wheel. Most vehicles today are also equipped with driver and passenger air bags that also aid in these areas of protection.

It is important to wear belts whether you are driving fast or slow. More than half of the crashes that cause injury or death happen at speeds less than forty miles per hour and within twenty-five miles from home.

The driver and front seat passengers must wear their seat belts. It is the law. The seat belt law applies to all passenger cars manufactured beginning with the nineteen sixty-eight models, and trucks beginning with the nineteen seventy-two year model.

It is unlawful for any person to operate a vehicle, in most states, unless every passenger of the vehicle under the age of eighteen is restrained by a safety belt or by a child restraint device regardless of seating positions.

If you asked most teens if they wear their seat belts, some would say they do not. Statistics are fairly high in all ethnic groups as the preceding graph reveals.

Teen Seat Belt Use

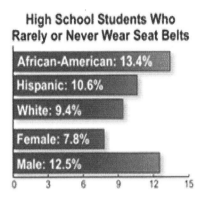

High School Students Who Rarely or Never Wear Seat Belts

African-American: 13.4%

Hispanic: 10.6%

White: 9.4%

Female: 7.8%

Male: 12.5%

Compared with other age groups, teens have the lowest rate of seat belt use. In 2005, 10.2% of high school students reported they rarely or never wear seat belts when riding with someone else.[v]

The law exempts the following from the seat belt requirement in most states:

(1) A person certified by a physician as having a medical condition that causes the seat belt use to be inappropriate or dangerous.

(2) Employees of a newspaper home delivery service while delivering newspapers or home delivery routes.

(3) School buses, buses used for transportation of persons for compensation, farm equipment, and trucks of a net weight of more than five thousand pounds.

If the passenger is eighteen years of age or older and fails to wear a seat belt, when required by law, the passenger will be charged with the violation.

The two life flight helicopters are on the scene to rescue five teenagers from a single vehicle crash. All passengers except one were wearing seatbelts. The next picture is another single vehicle crash in the same Alabama county just days apart. Fortunately all victims were not seriously injured.

PART NINE
RAILROAD CROSSINGS

A railroad crossing is where railway line is intersected by a road or any highway or street. When you are approaching a railroad crossing, you may see the red lights flashing and you may hear the train whistle blowing. These sights and sounds mean for you to apply your brakes in preparation to stop. This does **not** mean for you to accelerate and try to save a few minutes of time by not waiting for the train to pass

I am sure there have been times when the safety arm at the crossing failed to come down, and there may have been times when the red lights did not flash. However, in almost every crossing incident, the vehicle simply failed to stop. **Approximately 50% of all vehicles-train crashes occur at crossings with active warning devices.**

Safety tips for RR Crossings:

- First of all, always expect a train.
- Never race a train to the crossing even if you tie; you lose.
- Never get trapped on a crossing.
- When traffic is heavy you should wait until you are sure you can make the crossing before proceeding.
- When there is more than one track, always watch for the second train on another track.
- If the crossing arms are down, never drive around them.
- You should stay in your lane until the gates are raised.
- It is against the law to go around dropped crossing arms.
- If your vehicle has a manual transmission, shift down before you get to the crossing.
- Try to avoid changing gear on the tracks.
- Be prepared to stop if you are following a vehicle that is required to stop at crossings, such as trucks or buses.

If your vehicle stalls on a crossing, get everyone out of the vehicle immediately and away from the tracks as quickly as

possible. Call your local law enforcement agency for assistance.

More people in the United States die each year in highway-railroad crossing collisions than in all aviation crashes combined. It goes without saying that when a 3000 pound car and a train weighing several hundred tons meet, tragedy results.

NOTE: According to the US Department of Transportation there are about 5,800 vehicle train crashes each year in the United States. These collisions kill 600 people and injure about 2,300. More than 50% of all railroad fatal collisions occur at crossings with passive or inadequate safety devices (often none at all!). During daylight about 75% of car train collisions involve the train hitting the car, while at night about 50% of the time the car runs into the train! Drive safe! Expect the Unexpected at train crossings!

SCHOOL BUS LOADING AND UNLOADING

We should all respect the flashing red lights of the school bus when it stops to pick up or unload children. Never pass while the stop lights are flashing. This applies to four-lane highways as well. If the four lanes are divided by a center medium, the oncoming traffic is not normally required to stop.

In 2009, there were 221 fatal bus crashes in the U.S. (5% of total fatal crashes); 89 involved school buses, and 77 involved transit buses. More than 10,000 were injured.

THE HIGHWAY TRIO

Learn to listen to the highway trio sounds. They blend in perfect harmony. When you are tuned in, you will know your approximate speed without looking at your speed odometer. The highway trio is as follows: wind, road sound, and your engine. The wind makes a certain sound as it passes around your vehicle, depending on your speed. Your tires striking the pavement makes a different sound as you increase or slow your speed. Your engine revved up to the rpm speed of your choice makes yet another sound.

Listen and learn to identify these three different sounds. They will reveal your speed even without your looking. One should also develop their required senses while driving; hearing, feeling, touch, smell, and sight. Then, you will find yourself enjoying your drive without stress. This will also keep you alert if the engine should skip or start to show signs of less power than normal. This observation will also help one to drive at a steadier speed.

POINTS SYSTEM

All states have point systems in place for moving violations. **These points may vary from state to state.** Always check your local state point laws to know your rights. **Your license could be suspended when too many points build up against you.** Traffic school instruction courses will help eliminate points when ordered by the courts.

In Alabama, for Example, effective May 1, 2009, Points are assessed for various violations as follows:

- Any conviction which resulted from a charge that involved the drinking of alcoholic beverages and the driving of a motor vehicle but did not require mandatory revocation of the driver license...6 points
- Reckless driving or reckless endangerment involving operating a motor vehicle...............................6 points
- Failure to yield right-of-way...........................5 points
- Passing stopped school bus............................5 points
- Wrong side of road/illegal passing driving on the wrong side of the road or passing in an unauthorized passing zone..4 points

VALUABLE DRIVING TIPS

- Following too closely...................................3 points
- Disregarding traffic control devices...................3 points
- All other moving violations............................2 points
- Inability to control vehicle...........................2 points
  Allowing your vehicle to leave the designated right-of-way.
- Improper lane..2 points
- Speeding (1 to 25 mph over speed limit................2 points
- Speeding (26 or more mph over speed limit)...........5 points
- Drinking alcohol while operating a vehicle...........2 points
- Admin per se (a.k.a. DUI) This is a legal term for the process of when a police officer (admin), through one or more tests, determines that your Blood Alcohol Content (BAC) is over the state declared legal limit (per se) for driving; usually 0.08%................................6 points
- Improper operation of motorcycle.....................2 points
- Failure to obey construction/maintenance zone markers, flagman, police officer, or restricted lane............3 points
- Emergency vehicles (Not yielding to)..................2 points
- Fail to signal/use incorrect turn signal..............2 points
- Making improper turn..................................2 points
- Coasting (Shifting to neutral while going downhill).2 points

- Unsafe operation...2 points
- Texting while driving...................................2 points

You can lose your license by not following traffic laws. Offenses such as using a vehicle while committing a felony can also cause you to lose your license or have it suspended.

Suspension time is determined by the number of points gained during a specific period. The following list is used to determine the length of your suspension time:

12-14 points in a 2-year period: 60 days

15-17 points in a 2 year period: 90 days

18-20 points in a 2 year period: 120 days

21-23 points in a 2 year period: 180 days

24 points and more in a 2 year period: 365 days

In computing points and suspensions, the offense dates of all convictions are used. Three points will be deducted from the driver record of any person whose driving privilege has been suspended only once under the point system and has been reinstated, if such person has complied with all other requirements.

NOTE: Serving a point suspension does not prohibit these convictions from being used to accumulate additional suspensions or revocations.

These points may also vary from state to state. Before one attempts to impress friends with the performance of his vehicle, he/she should consider the points system.

TIPS FOR ALL

1. If you should drop something while driving, you should not try to retrieve it by reaching. One could pull on the steering wheel without realizing you are doing so resulting in losing control of the vehicle.

2. As we drive, we must never allow anything to impair our judgment or steal our focus and concentration from the road ahead.

3. Be a responsible driver. Give thought and consideration to other drivers.

4. Never, under any circumstances drive while under the influence of alcohol or drugs.

5. Never, under any circumstances, ride with anyone whom you think may be under these dangerous influences.

6. Never ride with a show-off driver. The life you are protecting is your very own.

7. Avoid backing into a busy street or highway to turn around.

8. Learn to hold a steady speed without cruise control.

9. Avoid using your brakes unnecessarily. Frequently tapping your brakes indicates a nervous or insecure driver.

10. Driving illegally can lead to an expensive experience. You could be carried to jail, your vehicle could be impounded, and you could face hundreds, or even thousands of dollars in unnecessary fees and fines. So why not do the right thing and be safe and responsible.

11. Help extend the life of your vehicle by changing the oil and filter and lubricating the chassis on a regular basis.

12. It is more difficult to judge the speed of on-coming traffic at night. Therefore, always be more cautious when turning left at night, passing through intersections, or entering the flow of traffic.

13. Always check your rearview and side mirrors before opening your door into the flow of traffic.

14. Before putting your vehicle in reverse always check to be sure your backing space is clear of pedestrians or debris. Do so even if your vehicle is equipped with motion sensors and/or backup cameras.

15. When riding in a vehicle your safety largely depends on the driving knowledge, experience and driving ability of the person at the wheel.

16. The driver of a pickup truck must always be very cautious when someone is riding in the cargo area. If there were a collision or crash of any kind those riding in the cargo area will have no protection from extreme danger.

One should never say, **"I don't want to get involved."** For safety reason we must all get involved in traffic safety. **If you see someone driving in a reckless manner, such as excessive speed, swerving, darting in and out of traffic, or typical showoff driving, you should report this action to the proper authorities.**

This does not make you a "snitch". It only shows you are concerned for human life. As a witness to careless driving, you are already involved. **Be responsible. Do the right thing. Your action could save a life.**

SPEED ALERT SYSTEM, AUTO LIFE GUARD

A silent eye is always watching your speed!

When you are learning to drive, or if you are experienced, remember this speed alert system may help to prevent further speeding tickets or automobile collisions.

conditions.

AMBER: A cautious driving speed which means you must keep a closer watch on road conditions and other drivers.

RED: GREEN: Usually a safe speed to drive under any normal road Red means "Danger!" There is no other way to say it!

For safety, these are a few of the vehicles we should NOT FOLLOW too closely, including hazardous loads. Following distances should not be closer than 150 feet if the speed limit is 50 mph or less. If the speed limit is 55 mph and above the following distance should not be closer than 300 feet.

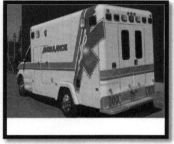

PART TEN

Alcohol and Drug Awareness

The Effect of Drugs and Alcohol on the Human Body and How It May Affect Your Driving Ability

To Maintain Good Health and Longevity:

Just Say No!

To Drugs and Alcohol

BLOOD ALCOHOL CONCENTRATIONS:

Alcohol begins to affect individuals prior to reaching the legally intoxicated Blood Alcohol Concentration level of .08%. If a 150 pound person consumes one drink equal to twelve ounces of beer (5% alcohol), five ounces of wine (12 % alcohol) or one-and-a-half ounces of hard liquor (40% alcohol), all would contain about the same amount of alcohol and would raise the person's Blood Alcohol Concentration about .02%. It takes the liver approximately one hour to oxidize or metabolize one drink.

Absorption: Alcohol is primarily absorbed through the stomach and the small intestines. It is considered a food because it has calories but, because it does not need to be digested, it proceeds directly into organs through the blood stream. **When the alcohol reaches the brain, impairment begins.** A greater amount of ingestion causes greater impairment to the brain, which, in turn, causes a person to have a greater degree of difficulty in functioning.

Metabolism/Elimination: The majority of alcohol in the body is eliminated by the liver. Ninety percent is eliminated through the body, while ten percent is eliminated (unchanged) through sweat and urine. Before the liver can process alcohol, a threshold amount is needed and can occur at the rate of one 12oz. can of beer, one 5 oz. glass of wine, or 1 ½ oz. shot of whiskey per hour.

Short-term Effects: Alcohol reduces sensitivity to pain. It affects vision in the following ways: narrows the visual field, reduces resistance to glare, interferes with the ability to differentiate intensities of light, and lessens sensitivity to colors.

Long Term Effects: Causes damage to vital organs; including liver, heart and pancreas. It is also linked to several medical conditions; including gastro intestinal problems, malnutrition, high blood pressure, and lower resistance to disease. **It is also linked to several types of cancer; including esophagus, stomach, liver, pancreas and colon.**

Drug Impact on Driving Skills: Impairment is related to alcohol, in terms of its concentration in the blood stream. **The brain's control of eye movements is highly vulnerable to alcohol. It only takes low to moderate blood alcohol concentrations (.03 to .05%) to interfere with voluntary eye movement and impair the eyes' ability to rapidly track a moving target.**

Steering an automobile is adversely affected by alcohol, as alcohol affects eye-to-hand reaction times, which are superimposed upon the visual effects. **Significant impairment and deterioration of steering ability begin at approximately .03 to .04% Blood Alcohol Concentrations and continue to deteriorate as Blood Alcohol Concentration rises.**

Almost every aspect of the brain's information-processing ability is impaired by alcohol. **Alcohol-impaired drivers require more time to read street signs or respond to traffic signals than unimpaired drivers.** Research on the effects of alcohol on the performance of automobile and aircraft operators shows a narrowing of the attention field beginning at .04% blood alcohol concentration.

Dividing Attention among Component Skills: Alcohol-impaired drivers who are required to divide their attention between two tasks tend to favor just one task. Often times the favored task is concentration on steering while becoming less vigilant with respect to other safety information. **Numerous studies indicate that divided attention deficits occur as low as .02% Blood Alcohol Concentration.**

Differences between Abuse and Dependence: Alcohol dependency and alcohol abusers experience many of the same harmful effects of drinking. The critical difference is the physical dependence displayed by alcoholics and their lack of ability to regulate their consumption of alcohol. Alcoholics will continue to drink in spite of severe negative consequences of their drinking.

Warning Signs of Problem Drinking:

- Frequently drinking to state of intoxication.
- Using alcohol to seek relief from problems and cope with stress.
- Engaging in antisocial behavior during and after drinking.
- Going to work intoxicated or decline in job performance.
- Experiencing family or economic problems.
- Driving a car under the influence of alcohol.
- Sustaining injuries as a result of intoxication.
- Seeking out places where alcohol is available and avoiding places where it is not.

ALCOHOLISM:

Alcoholism is a primary, chronic disease with genetic, psychosocial, and environmental factors influencing its development and manifestations. The disease is often progressive and fatal. It is characterized by continuous or periodic impaired control over drinking, preoccupation with drug alcohol, use of alcohol despite adverse consequences, and distortions in thinking-most notable denial.

Definition of Addiction: Physiological and/or psychological dependence on a drug. The overpowering physical or emotional urge to repeatedly do something that is uncontrollable by the individual and is accompanied by a tolerance for the drug, with withdrawal symptoms if the drug is stopped.

STAGES OF ADDICTION:

Addiction develops in predictable series of stages:

Early Stage Addiction: It is characterized by an increase in tolerance and dependence. People who are becoming addicted can use larger and larger quantities without becoming intoxicated or suffering harmful consequences.

As the body cells change to tolerate larger quantities of the chemical, even larger quantities are needed to achieve the same effect. **It is difficult to distinguish addictive use from heavy non-addictive use because there are few outward symptoms. Alcohol or drugs are used so frequently that the person comes to depend on them.** Use begins to seem normal; life without use begins to seem abnormal.

Middle Stage Addiction: It is marked by a progressive loss of control. It takes more alcohol or drugs to get high. Increased quantities damage the liver, alter brain chemistry, and eventually, tolerance begins to decrease. The drug is used to relieve the pain created by not using. Physical, psychological, and social problems develop.

Chronic Stage Addiction: It is marked by physical, psychological, behavioral, social, and spiritual deterioration. All systems of the body can be affected.

Mood swings are common as the person uses the drug to feel better, but cannot maintain the good feelings. There is less and less control over behavior. Relationships are damaged and the person loses touch with a higher power and loses the sense of purpose and meaning in life. Therefore, life is consumed with the need to use.

FACTORS THAT AFFECT:

Absorption/Metabolism/Elimination

A person's weight and the total amount of body fat determine the outcome on the drug's total effect on the body. The more body fat the slower the drug is consumed. Also, the aging process affects the manner in which the drug exerts its effects on the body. The older a person is the faster he or she will get drunk.

The biomedical/chemical makeup of each individual tolerates substances differently. For example: a person' physical condition as well as hypersensitivity (allergies) or hyposensitivity (need for larger doses to gain the desired effect) will influence the total effect of the drug on the individual. Each drug metabolizes or processes within the body at a different rate. The drug remains active in the body until metabolism occurs. For example: certain medications require dosages to be taken every four, twelve or twenty-four hours, depending on the duration and rate at which the drug is metabolized.

Food: If a person has eaten a meal and then begins to drink or do drugs the body slows absorption of the drug into the body by not allowing it to pass directly through the digestive process without first being processed by the digestive system. A slower process occurs, since the body is digesting food in addition to the substance or drug utilized by the person.

Emotional factors may influence drug absorption and metabolism within the body. A person's specific emotional state or degree of psychological comfort or discomfort will influence how a drug may affect the individual. For example, if a person began using alcohol and was extremely angry or upset, the alcohol could intensify this anger or psychological discomfort. On the other hand, if alcohol was being used as part of a celebration, the psychological state of pleasure could be enhanced by the use of the drug.

The degree of anticipation or expectancy to which a person believes that a given drug will affect them may have an effect on their emotional state. If a person truly believes that by using a substance, they will experience a given effect, then their expectations may cause a psychological change in the manner in which the drug affects them.

The method of administration, tolerance and the presence or use of other drugs is a determining factor. A drug injected directly into the blood stream will affect an individual at a greater rate, since it will be directly absorbed through the blood stream and presented to various organs. If a drug is snorted or inhaled, the effects may be enhanced, due to the fact that the sinus cavity is located in close proximity to the brain. On the other hand, if a drug is ingested, the effects may be slower due to the fact that they must pass through the digestive system.

Tolerance refers to the amount of a given substance necessary to receive its desired effect. If a person is physically addicted to a drug, then more of a given substance may be necessary and the effects on the body will differ from those seen in a non-dependent individual. The presence or use of other drugs will also influence the rate of absorption and metabolism of drugs in the body.

FACTS ABOUT DRINKING, DRIVING AND DRUGS:

Here is a staggering fact: the leading causes of teenage deaths are automobile collisions. It has been well documented that automobile crashes are responsible for more than 40,000 fatalities every year in the United States! Many of these victims are inexperienced and irresponsible teenage drivers.

High speed, following too closely, and inexperienced drivers are the reasons for some of these highway collisions. However, the most devastating cause of automobile crashes is the detrimental impact of alcohol and drugs. **Young people who drink and drive may be particularly at risk for being involved in a motor vehicle collision because they have less experience with driving, and are more likely to engage in risk-taking behavior.**

Alcohol is a depressant drug, which means it slows down your brain and body. Other depressant drugs, including some prescription drugs such as sedatives and painkillers, affect a person's ability to drive safely, in a way similar to effects of alcohol. Any drug that causes drowsiness, including some cough, cold, or allergy medications, can also affect a person's ability to drive safely. **Even if you only drink a little alcohol your**

chances of being in a crash is much greater than if you did not drink at all. No one can drink alcohol or do drugs and drive safely. It is also true if one has been driving for many years. Young drivers are more affected by alcohol because their body is still in the growth process and their liver has not developed to the extent that they can efficiently process the alcohol in their blood stream.

 When Alcohol and other depressant drugs are combined, the effects are more intense and dangerous than the effect of either drug on its own.

THE REASON WE SAY—"JUST SAY NO":

Alcohol can be very dangerous when mixed with other recreational drugs and medication. Alcohol and drugs slow down reflexes, impair judgment, and can blur vision. Alcohol and drugs prevent you from hearing sounds normally, affect your concentration, and cause loss of coordination. They also often promote anger and over confidence.

In regards to teenage personal academic abilities, research shows teenagers who do drugs and alcohol **score lower** than their nonparticipating peers on vocabulary, their ability to perceive normality of the mind's eye, memory tests and are more likely to **perform poorly** in school as a whole. **Teens that use drugs and alcohol may remember 10 percent less of what they learned compared to non-users!** Teenagers who drink and use drugs are **four times more likely** than their non-user peers **to suffer from depression**!

Some laws regarding impaired driving apply to people who serve alcohol, whether it is in a public place, such as a restaurant or bar, or in a private home. For example, if you had a party and one of your guests drove away after drinking too much and caused an automobile crash, you could be sued for damages. Everyone who serves alcohol has the responsibility to ensure that his or her patrons or guests do not get behind the wheel after drinking too much.

When one considers the penalty for drinking and driving, one should make sure he or she never gets themselves put in that position. **The penalty for a first conviction could be between 600 and 2,100 dollars, and up to one year in jail, or, both fine and jail.** In addition, the driver's license could be suspended for ninety days. For the second conviction, the third, and the forth, the fine can be as much as 10,000 dollars resulting in a class "C" felony and a five year revocation of driver's license, additionally, the offender may be imprisoned for not less than one year and one day, or, not more than ten years.

 Alcohol related collisions have killed more people than all the U.S. soldiers ever killed in war. Think before you drink and drive!

Some state laws may vary when considering the legal consumption of alcohol while driving on our public highways. The State of Alabama says that, for drivers over 21, the level of .08% Blood Alcohol Content (BAC) and above is the unlawful level to drive. **A person under the age of 21 can be considered DUI if his or her blood alcohol level is .02% BAC or higher!** Commercial carriers can be charged with a DUI at .04% or more.

Think you can just refuse to take a DUI test? Think again! When you signed forms to apply for a driver's license, you agreed to comply with requests by law enforcement officers to take chemical testing to determine your blood-alcohol content (BAC). Chemical testing includes breath, oral swab, blood, and urine testing.

A breath test or mouth swab can be administered roadside or at any location; blood and urine testing can only be performed at a medical facility or detention facility.

Road-side Test

WHAT IS IMPLIED CONSENT:

All states have 'implied consent laws' that come into effect when you are tested for BAC if it is over .08 percent or if you refuse to take a chemical test for BAC when requested by a police officer. In some states you may even find this information in the fine print on your driver's license. The laws you are subjected to are those of the state in which you were arrested, not the state where you obtained your driver's license

If you are stopped by a law enforcement officer and you refuse a breath test or mouth swab test for alcohol and chemical substances, your license could be suspended under the implied consent law.

The implied consent law states that any person who accepts the privilege of operating a motor vehicle within the state is, by so operating such vehicle, deemed to have given his or her consent to submit to an approved chemical test or physical test.

These tests include, but are not limited to, an infrared light test of his or her breath for the purpose of determining the alcoholic content of his or her blood or breath, if the person is lawfully arrested for any offense allegedly committed while the person was driving or was in actual physical control of a motor vehicle while under the influence of alcoholic beverages.

Additionally, this law stipulates that, in DUI cases involving serious bodily injury or death, an officer may use reasonable force if necessary to require the driver to submit to the administration of a blood test. Even if you refuse, reasonable force may be used to draw blood for a BAC test under these circumstances.

Implied consent laws include:

- Producing a driver's license and proof of insurance when asked.
- Consenting to blood, oral swab, urine, or breathe tests to determine your blood alcohol content if requested.
- Performing field sobriety tests if requested.

Tests for Intoxication include:

- Blood Analysis. The methodology of blood analysis measures the amount of percentage of alcohol per 1,000 drops of blood.
- Breathe Analysis. Measures the blood alcohol content of air in the lungs.
- Urinalysis. Detects marijuana, cocaine, PCP, and heroin; and gives the presence of the drug. It does not provide the level of impairment, since legal levels of impairment have not been established.

Marijuana opponents claim that marijuana causes major Impairments and that any use while driving can lead to increased automobile crashes and fatalities. Using alcohol with marijuana can decrease your motor-skill control, your mental concentration, and greatly impair your ability to drive.

ALCOHOL POISONING:

The human body is an amazing creation and has many built in defense systems. One such defense system is a defense against the body being fatally poisoned by alcohol. A person's body has a "threshold" where this defense system takes action. This threshold varies from person to person depending on many factors such as weight, age, ability to metabolize alcohol, etc.

When this defense system kicks in, you are on the verge of fatally poisoning your body with alcohol. The action that the body takes in its defense is not a pleasant one. A drastic action (ingesting this amount of alcohol) requires and equally drastic reaction! **The body reacts by causing you to regurgitate, or "throw up" the contents of your stomach!** Not pretty, huh?

Not that we need one, but another good reason to avoid mixing alcohol and drugs is because marijuana and other chemical drugs suppress the gag reflex which means you may not be able to "throw up" the excess alcohol when your body needs to do so.

Alcohol, drugs and gasoline do not mix. If you choose to engage in such dangerous activities as using drugs and/or alcohol, you must not drive! Don't risk the lives of others just because you don't value and respect your own life!

How long do drugs and alcohol stay in the system? **The length of time any drug (illicit or prescribed) stays in your system will vary.** In large part, it depends on your physiological makeup (e.g., your physical height, weight, amount of body fat, your age, current state of health, whether or not you exercise mildly, aggressively, or at all). Whether or not you are undergoing any degree of stress and your state of mind at the time you ingest drugs or alcohol into the body play a part as well.

While driver education programs and highway safety tests emphasize the importance of safe driving habits, young drivers are too often unaware of the serious consequences of driving their automobile under the influence of alcohol and drugs which cause reckless driving behavior.

IF I DRINK COFFEE, I'LL SOBER UP, RIGHT:

Ever hear a person ask, "Is there a way to sober up quickly?" The answer is NO! Once a person consumes alcohol, it enters the bloodstream and only time can reduce the concentration of alcohol in the blood.

With three, maybe four DUI's or more, one could be grounded for a life time. A bad record induced with drugs and alcohol could keep you from obtaining a passport for travel outside the United States; or it may disqualify you from that all important job.

The most frightening thoughts are; your first experience with illicit drugs could be irreversible. If you are involved in an automobile collision where you are at fault that results in the death of another person, you could be facing a vehicular manslaughter charge.

The four leading cause of automobile collisions are alcohol, drugs, speed and distractions. Think before you use drugs or alcohol and drive a vehicle. It really is your life. Protect it.

The Long Term Effects of Drinking, Driving and Drugs

Ever hear of people having problems gaining or losing weight because of how fast or slow their metabolism may be? Just like people having different metabolisms for food, each person has a different metabolism for chemical drugs and alcohol.

It takes about an hour for the average human body to process and eliminate (metabolize) two-thirds of the alcohol in one standard drink. This rate is constant, meaning that the more you drink the longer time you need to wait before driving.

Drinking coffee or other caffeinated beverages may make you slightly more alert temporarily, but your ability to drive will still be impaired.

DUI Awareness Test Question

1) The best highway safety insurance that you can have is the _____ you keep between you and the vehicle in front of you.

2) There are three types of common road signs. They are: Regulatory, Warning, and _____.

You may be driving too close to the vehicle in front of you if you can read the tag number when traveling at _____ mph.

Your license could be suspended if you are stopped by law enforcement agents and you refuse a sobriety test. True _____, False _____

Drugs, alcohol and speed are a leading cause of automobile collisions. True _____, False _____

The greater your speed becomes, the lighter your vehicle becomes; therefore, reducing your ability to stay in full control. True _____, False _____

Hand held electronic devices should never be used while driving. True _____, False _____

Speed limit signs are posted to tell you how fast you must drive. True _____, False _____

9) A mandatory liability insurance requirement is in place and proof of such insurance must be carried in the vehicle at all times. True_____, False_____

10) The leading cause of teenage deaths between the age of 15 and 19 are _____

11) The first experience with illegal drugs could be irreversible. True _____, False _____

12) A person under the age of 21 years can be charged with a DUI if their blood alcohol level is _____ or more.

13) The penalty for a first conviction could be between _____ and _____dollars, and up to one year in jail, or, both fine and jail.

14) Teenagers who use drugs and alcohol may remember_____% less than the non-user of drugs and alcohol.

15) When under the influence of alcohol; drinking coffee or other caffeinated beverages may temporarily make you more alert, but your ability to drive will still be impaired. True _____, False _____

16) The brain's control of eye movements is highly vulnerable to alcohol at the level of (.03 to .05). True_____, False_____

17) Alcohol impaired drivers require more time to read street signs or respond to traffic signals than non-alcohol-impaired drivers. True_____, False_____

8) Young people who drink and drive may be particularly at risk for being involved in a motor vehicle collision because_____ _____ _____

9) What is Alcoholism? _____

_____

20) How does alcohol affect the body with long term use?

_____

21) Alcohol begins to affect a person's steering ability of an automobile at approximately what level? _____

22) Alcohol impaired drivers who are required to divide their attention between two task tend to favor just one task. True_____False_

23) Alcoholism is a disease and is often _____.

24) List some of the effects of the chronic stage of addiction._____

_____

25) Even if you only drink a little alcohol, your chances of being in a crash are much greater than if you did not drink at all.

True_____ False _____

26) What is alcohol intolerance? _____

For the test answers, use a separate sheet of paper. Answer the questions by numbers in order only. Write down numbers 1-26. If you cannot answer a question, skip that number by making an "X" by the number and move on to the next question. This method will keep your answers in the correct order.

If you marked an X by a number you must go back and restudy. All questions must be answered correctly in order to pass the course.

Always check your local state laws to be familiar with any mandatory and state requirements which may affect your driving responsibility.

The resource information in this book has been taken in part from the following websites and from the author's experience and observation while driving over 4 million collision free miles.

www.cdc.gov

www.nida.nih.gov

http://www.nhtsa.gov

http://en.wikipedia.org/wiki/NationalHighway_Traffic_Safety_Admi nistration

http://www-nrd.nhtsa.dot.gov

http://www.census.gov

http://www.edgarsnyder.com/motorcycle-accident/statistics.html

http://www.jmu.edu/safetyplan/vehicle/generaldriver.shtml

www.cdc.gov/Motorvehiclesafety/Teen_Drivers

Statistics from various websites may vary to some degree. Pictures were, in part, courtesy of *Clay Times Journal*, the author's collection and various websites.

My thanks and gratitude goes to these people who have helped make this book possible:

Michael and Cynthia Halfmann, Candy McDonald

James Deleo (aka) Delta DJ, Allan Garich

Linda Williams, Ryan Carter, Vonda Easly

Literary Adviser: Charla Coleman-Deleo

Editor: Greg Hindmon

This book was hand written by Ralph Moore
and transferred to type by Annette Carter

Address:

Valuable Driving Tips

P.O. Box 857

Lineville, AL 36266

Web Site:

www.vdt-info.com

Email:

valuabledrivingtips@gmail.com

[i]Natural learning-valuable driving tips for beginners and professionals. (p.6). Retrieved from http://en.wikipedia.org/wiki/NationalHighway_Traffic_Safety_Administration/

[ii]Natural learning-valuable driving tips for beginners and professionals. (p. 20). Retrieved from www.cdc.gov/Motorvehiclesafety/

[iii]Natural learning-valuable driving tips for beginners and professionals. (p. 21). Retrieved from http://www.cdc.gov/Motorvehiclesafety/Teen_Drivers/

[iv]Natural learning-valuable driving tips for beginners and professionals. (p. 66). Retrieved from http://www-fars.nhtsa.dot.gov/

[v]Natural learning - valuable driving tips for beginners and professionals. (p. 139). Retrieved from www.cdc.gov/Motorvehiclesafety/Teen_Drivers

Notes